AT HOME IN THE BIBLE

AT HOME IN THE BIBLE

BY

T. H. DARLOW, M.A.

HODDER AND STOUGHTON LTD.

TORONTO   LONDON   NEW YORK

1923

Made and Printed in Great Britain.
Hazell, Watson & Viney, Ld., London and Aylesbury.

TO

ALL MY FELLOW-SERVANTS IN

THE BIBLE SOCIETY,

AT HOME AND ABROAD—AND ABOVE.

Foreword

THE following brief meditations are reprinted from *The Bible in the World*, the monthly organ of the Bible Society. That catholic organization brings together Christian men and women of many schools—both ecclesiastical and theological. The editor of its magazine has felt bound therefore to avoid questions about which his readers would disagree, and to confine himself to the elemental truths and experiences concerning which faithful folk can be of one mind and heart. In their collected form, these papers may provide one more illustration of the truth that the things which divide us are temporal, but the things which unite us are eternal.

T. H. DARLOW,

For twenty-five years Literary Superintendent of the British and Foreign Bible Society.

THE BIBLE HOUSE, 146 QUEEN VICTORIA STREET, LONDON.
January 1923.

Contents

Contents

HEINE pronounced the Bible to be the homeliest of books. At least we can say with confidence that in no other book is it possible for us to become so profoundly and entirely at home. Such a result, however, implies in the first place patient reading and careful study. For example, to be at home in Shakespeare means, at any rate, that you know the plots of the plays, you have made friends with the characters, you can recognize their words in a quotation. Now in the same kind of way we ought to grow versed in the varied content of Scripture until its patriarchs and saints and prophets seem to us old familiar faces, and we recognize by instinct the habit of an apostle's thought and the turn of an evangelist's phrase. To have our minds and memories saturated with the words of Holy Writ can beget transforming results even in our common speech. Concerning a preacher in the twelfth century, J. M. Neale declared that " he seems to quote the Bible, because it is his own natural language, because his thoughts have been so accustomed to flow in Scripture channels that they will run in no other ; and it is sometimes difficult to tell, nor would he perhaps always have known himself, whether he was employing his own words or those of the inspired writings.'' In modern days the two greatest speakers of the English tongue have been beyond question Abraham Lincoln and John Bright, and with both men their style was born out of life-long familiarity with the Bible. The sacred language of Scripture '' doth breed perpetual benediction,'' when it rises in sacred moments to the lips of those who love it. Sometimes in a village prayer-meeting we have marvelled at unlettered ploughmen and shepherds who spoke with God in the awful and glorious words of revelation—words which they had learned to use freely and naturally as the true vernacular of the soul.

For the Bible contains both the grammar and the vocabulary of the universal Christian language. It is wonderful how believers of unlike races, in lands and ages far removed, can meet and communicate and hold converse together in this holy mother-tongue. Men as wide apart as Augustine and Bunyan and Gordon are intelligible to one another, for they all use the *lingua franca* of the saints. To be nurtured in God's Book is to understand the common speech of God's whole family in heaven and on earth. And the fact that each lover of the Bible becomes at home in its spiritual dialect forms one among many latent tokens that the real reunion of Christendom lies nearer than we sometimes dream.

We have a proverb which warns us that familiarity will breed contempt ; but this only happens when we grow familiar with things which are in their essence trivial or vulgar or base. Familiarity with Nature herself breeds no contempt, but strange veneration and affection. Each of us can probably recall certain places on earth which for him seem haunted with peculiar tenderness. Among the meadows round his ancestral homestead, a grey-haired farmer will look fondly at the grassy footpaths which he has trodden ever since he was a child. And for an old disciple the same deep emotions cluster round the chapters of Holy Writ. In those green pastures he has been at home all his life through. He can never miss his track along the immemorial pathway of promise and consolation. This passage was the first he learned to spell at his mother's knee. This was the psalm they sang over his father's grave. This single text shone out like a star through the midnight of doubt and dismay, and sealed upon his spirit the peace which passeth all understanding. So it comes about that to a Christian the pages of his pocket Bible are crimsoned as with a tincture of all that has been most deep-felt and impassioned in the experience of the past. The faded little volume, with its well-worn cover, is a reliquary which enshrines his dearest and holiest secrets, a register which records how God has dealt with his soul. Thus Christians discover that, alike in a human

and in a Divine sense, the Bible is the book of
life.

Yet to say no more than this would be to fall
far short of the truth. Can you ever feel entirely
at home, except in the company of the persons
whom you love best ? It is the supreme beatitude of Scripture that it introduces us into the
very presence and company of the Crucified.
To believing hearts the whole Book grows instinct and alive with Him, Whom having not
seen they love. The wind bloweth where it
listeth, but each breeze among the branches
of this tree of life whispers the Name that
is above every name. Each prophet fastens
eager eyes upon His advent, and each apostle
bears witness to His glory, and each martyr
rejoices to suffer for His sake. Those who know
the Bible best learn that it has no speech nor
language where His voice is not heard. Through
its chapters *Cor ad cor loquitur*, the Redeemer
holds converse with His redeemed. Thus it
comes to pass that for soldiers in foreign trenches,
for stricken men on lonely beds of pain, for
prisoners and exiles who are homeless in a
strange land, this Book has mysterious power
to re-create home in the heart. Those who
read it by the waters of Babylon discover that
they are come unto Mount Zion unawares. For
to those who use it aright the Bible proves nothing less than a sacrament of Jesus Christ Himself. There they behold His sacred Face in
almost every page. And so we cease to wonder

that the truest Christians should speak with such reverence and affection of their Book ; because in that Book, as in no other place or way, they find themselves at home—at home with the Lord.

THE SPARROW HATH FOUND AN HOUSE

THERE are some experiences which never grow stale by repetition. They recur continually, without losing their fresh wonder and zest. Year after year the earth grows young again when, by the miracle of springtime, once more the heavenly Power makes all things new. Nature, having been planted in the likeness of death, is found again in the likeness of resurrection. This is the Lord's doing ; and each year it is more marvellous in our eyes. Surely the Rabbis had a true instinct when they decided that the world must have been created in spring.

At such a season, " when sparrows build and the leaves break forth," it is not difficult to obey Christ's commandment, and to consider the birds of the air. Indeed, few of His comfortable sayings are more full of comfort than the lesson which He bade us learn from the sparrows. In His day these little birds were just as common and just as cheap as they are in England now. In the market of modern Jerusalem fowlers still offer for sale strings of larks and sparrows, which are used as food by the poor. " Are not

two sparrows sold for a farthing ? and not one
of them shall fall to the ground without your
Father." No preacher has ventured to affirm
the doctrine of a special Providence so absolutely
as Jesus Christ. " The Lord upholdeth all that
fall," sang the Psalmist—yea, even those tiny,
twittering birds which men consider hardly
worth stooping to pick up. The Divine thought
is so great that nothing seems small in His sight.
The Father's heart is so wide that it takes the
humblest of His creatures in.

The vast majority of men and women resemble
sparrows in this, that they are intensely commonplace. The Persian poet likened God to a
chess-player, who moves His human pieces
across this chequer-board of nights and days.
But in actual life the kings and queens and
bishops are few and far apart, while the pawns
make up a huge, indistinguishable army. Most
people seem marked out by nothing except their
extreme mediocrity. They are painfully alike.
The average man may be respectable ; he is
certainly not romantic. He seems dull to nearly
every one, except of course to himself. We may
be certain that many of our acquaintances consider us quite as uninteresting as we consider
them—and on equally good grounds. " Such a
very ordinary person ! " Yes, most men are very
ordinary. Even their vices are commonplace.
Cheap meanness and stupid sloth and vulgar
passion and fustian selfishness—these are the sins
which drag average people down to perdition.

The Gospel reveals the immeasurable value which the meanest, dullest human creature possesses in the eyes of Almighty God. We call such a person " uninteresting." God has an intense and tireless interest in every single soul which He made originally in His own likeness, and endowed with the awful gift of choice, and kindled with a spark of immortality. God watches over that soul with personal solicitude, as though the rest of His universe were not the same to Him as that one poor, commonplace human unit. God has set His love upon that solitary soul. He covets its affection, as if in some way it could complete His own beatitude. To Him it has a mysterious preciousness, of which redemption is the measure and the pledge.

When we are most tempted to lose heart because of our own insignificance and helplessness, the Gospel bids us be of good cheer as we remember the sparrows. The loneliest, feeblest, forlornest man can find refuge and rest in this revelation of the personal, unspeakable, inexplicable love of God. Though he knows himself to be contemptible and insignificant and guilty— a creature of no account—the God who knows him far better than he knows himself sees something in him worth loving. God prizes him unspeakably, He gives him a place and portion in His eternal love. *The sparrow hath found an house;* and here the shelterless soul can dwell safely, in peace that passeth all understanding.

Thus the Bible appeals to the most commonplace persons, and speaks to them in the homeliest way. And so faithful folk who are very simple and dull and unlettered nevertheless find themselves at home in the Book of God. The poor of this world obtain the franchise of Scripture, and hold the keys of its treasury. It is strange and beautiful to note how some humble believer, quite untaught in men's wisdom, can become domesticated in God's household and initiated into the mysteries of the kingdom of heaven. The sacred and glorious words of Scripture pass naturally into his prayers. When he speaks face to face with the Father in secret, he uses the language of the apostles and prophets. With happy confidence, with holy familiarity, such an one enters the sanctuary of Scripture, and stands in the presence-chamber of the great King—" no more a stranger or a guest, but like a child at home."

THE BOOK WHICH IS ALIVE

In a speech which he once delivered at the Royal Academy Banquet, Mr. Rudyard Kipling delighted his distinguished audience by a parable concerning the origin of literature. " There is an ancient legend which tells us that when a man first achieved a most notable deed, he wished to explain to his tribe what he had done. As soon as he began to speak, however, he was smitten with dumbness, he lacked words, and sat down.

Then there arose—according to the story—a masterless man, one who had taken no part in the action of his fellow, who had no special virtues, but was afflicted with the magic of the necessary words. He saw, he told, he described the merits of the notable deed in such a fashion, we are assured, that *the words became alive and walked up and down in the hearts of all his hearers.* Thereupon, the tribe seeing that the words were certainly alive, and fearing lest the man with the words would hand down untrue tales about them to their children, they took and killed him. But later they saw that the magic was in the words, not in the man."

We need not go on with the legend. To Christians it suggests an irresistible application. There is one Book, above all others in the world, of which we may say that its words become alive and walk up and down in the hearts of its hearers. Long ago a wise king set forth this strange, un-earthly effect in phrases which are always coming true : " When thou goest, it shall lead thee ; when thou sleepest, it shall keep thee ; and when thou awakest, it shall talk with thee." We do not account for such a result, when we ascribe it to " the magic of the necessary words." The spiritual charm and potency of Scripture refuse to be explained as literature. Christians confess that holy men of old spake as they were moved by the Holy Ghost. Often these prophets and apostles were persecuted and killed. But their words are deathless ; and that most

notable deed, whose merits they describe, is
nothing less than the redeeming work of the
love of God.

We recognize that a book is alive when it
touches our modern needs and hopes and
problems, when it appeals to the people of
to-day. Yet vitality does not mean novelty.
Discussing the art and influence of Ibsen, *The
Times* declared that the Norwegian dramatist
will have a deeper meaning for each generation—
a meaning which the labours of modern students
have done something to bring to light, but which
future ages will certainly grasp more and more
fully—a meaning which no changes in society or
belief can put out of date. In a far profounder
sense we claim that no changes in society or
belief can put the Bible out of date. It is just
as modern to-day, and just as living, as it was a
thousand years ago, and as it will be a thousand
years hence. Even though a whole generation
of mankind should fall asleep to its eternal
message, yet we could still say confidently :
" When thou awakest, it shall talk with
thee."

The converse which the Bible holds with men
is not only vital but personal. Amid all the
countless complexities of human nature and
human life, the Spirit there speaks to each individual—the aged saint, the despairing penitent,
the happy child. It answers to every mood of
the inward man, and touches humanity at all
points. It understands my condition, and sym-

pathizes with my doubts and troubles and joys.
"This Book has been through all my experience;
somehow or other it talks with me as if it were a
fellow-pilgrim." No other literature in the
world is half so intimate as the awful revelation
of God.

Again, the Bible talks to us in the most
practical fashion. It speaks in simple words,
which come home to plain people—as though
God laid aside high, celestial speech, so that
He might condescend to men of low estate and
communicate with us in the earth-born *patois* of
our native land. His Gospel comes not with
enticing words of man's wisdom, but in demon-
stration of the Spirit and in power. And the
mighty sayings of the Scripture still have power
to become alive and walk about in the hearts of
its readers and hearers. Of no book except the
Bible do Mr. Kipling's phrases come completely
true. But bare words from the Bible can still
lead nations into or out of captivity, can open
to us the doors of other worlds, can stir us so
intolerably that we can scarcely abide to look
at our own souls. As a great modern preacher
puts it : " Why, the Book has wrestled with
me ; the Book has smitten me ; the Book has
comforted me ; the Book has smiled on me ;
the Book has frowned on me ; the Book has
clasped my hand ; the Book has warmed my
heart. The Book weeps with me and sings
with me ; it whispers to me and it preaches to
me ; it maps my way and holds up my goings,

It is a live Book ; from its first chapter to its last word it is full of a strange, mystic vitality."

THE LORD SHEWED HIM ALL THE LAND

No explorer has identified the exact peak which Moses climbed that he might gaze over all the Land of Promise before he died. It may be said, indeed, that the whole range of the hills of Moab forms one vast Pisgah, from which your sight crosses the deep cleft of the Jordan valley at your feet and explores the prospect of Canaan that spreads out beyond. There are some mountain-top experiences which never fade from a man's memory—when, for example, he stands on an Alpine summit which overlooks the watershed of Europe, and marks how on this side the streams of melting snow make their way northward to join the Rhine, while on that side they drain down into the Danube and flow eastward to mix with the Black Sea. To-day, indeed, we have no need to climb a mountain : we can get glimpses of what a whole country looks like by means of the photographs which are taken from aeroplanes. They help us, for the first time, to conceive for ourselves " that variegated mosaic of the world's surface which a bird sees in its migration, that difference between the lands of the gentian and of the olive which the stork and the swallow see afar off, as they lean upon

the sirocco wind." Now these things are an
allegory—to remind us how often we fail and fall
short, by reason of our contracted spiritual
vision. So many Christians exist with hardly
any proper horizon. Their sympathies are
shut in by the walls of their family tent, their
outlook is bounded by the limits of their ecclesiastical camp. They never gain a Pisgah sight
of Palestine, they cannot measure the spacious
inheritance of the Israel of God.

This principle holds good in regard to reading
the Bible. There are not a few students of
God's Book who keep their eyes so close to its
pages that they fail to grasp the Divine purport
of the whole. They are like students of painting
who judge some great picture by poring over a
few selected square inches of the canvas. These
microscopic readers pore over the jots and tittles
of Scripture until they lose their sense of its
perspective and proportion. They concentrate
on this corner or that corner, but they never see
all the land. Textual criticism has its own
value. For the sake of minute accuracy our
English revisers adopted about twenty thousand
changes in the text of the Greek Testament.
Yet the bulk of these alterations were quite
trivial, and the whole of them, taken together,
made no perceptible difference to the total message of the Evangelists and the Apostles. Without being critics, many Christians miss their way
in the Bible, because they pay attention to so
little beyond their favourite passages. But

we cannot possibly grasp the power of an Epistle
or a Gospel by picking out those verses which
appeal to us, regardless of the setting in which
they occur and from which they must not be
torn away. Bishop Westcott was a meticulous
commentator on each word and syllable of the
New Testament. Yet before he began a course
of lectures on the Epistle to the Hebrews—which
lasted for a year and then was left unfinished—
he urged his students to start by reading the
whole Epistle straight through for themselves
three or four times over, so that they might grasp
the main drift of its argument and trace the
thread which runs through its successive para-
graphs. Many devout readers of the Bible lose
enormously because they hardly ever sit down
and quietly read one of its books straight
through. We cannot enter into the school of the
Prophets or the Apostles unless we let their message tell upon our minds with full, unbroken force.

The same truth applies to Scripture as a
whole. John Stuart Mill referred with a touch
of sarcasm to those people who fancy that the
Bible is all one book. It is a great mistake to
do so ; but, as a profounder teacher than Mill has
confessed, it is perhaps a still greater mistake
to think that the Bible is *not* one book, or that
it has no unity. " What fascinates me in the
Bible is not a passage here and there, not something which only a scholar or an antiquarian can
detect in it, but the Bible as a whole." One in-
creasing revelation runs through all its long

centuries of record. The Gospel of God's righteousness and redemption, which was spoken at
sundry times and in divers manners, at last
grows explicit and articulate in the Person of His
Son. But the end of the Bible looks backward
to its beginning. And we can never appropriate
the fullness of our heritage in Holy Scripture
unless the Lord shows us all the land.

We might go on to show how this principle
applies also to the study of Christian doctrine
and the history of Christian society. In both
these fields we suffer continually on account of
our narrow, parochial, provincial outlook. We
fall into the snare of the specialist who con-
centrates on details so that he loses sight of the
total reality. When an American talks about
" God's country," he commonly means his own
particular bit of the world, the place where he
was bred and born. And to any good man that
place ought to appear holy ground : but it
is only one tiny corner of God's country. A
wonderful thing happened at the Lambeth
Conference when the assembled bishops were
carried away in spirit to the top of a high mountain, where they had a vision of the Great Church
which embraces all smaller Churches in its bosom.
Reunion will become possible when the Lord
shows us all the land. Moreover, in our poor
human estimate of God's kingdom on earth and
the effect of the Gospel among men, we are apt
to forget that the Gospel treats this present life
as after all a mere fragment of the life of the

world to come.   Things would seem far otherwise, could we but climb where Moses stood
and view the landscape of immortality.

THE WELL IS DEEP

WHEN we first begin to read the Bible, we
are moving about in worlds not realized.
And we fared in the same fashion when we had
to read the old Greek and Latin authors, as
boys at school.   We could not possibly perceive
how much the classics contained.   It is only
in after years, when a lad has grown older and
gained some experience and learned what life
means and felt for himself what Virgil calls
" the sense of tears in mortal things "—it is
only then that lines and pages learned by rote
come back to him and pierce him with their
sad reality.   They speak the universal experience of mankind with a voice like the voice
of Nature herself ;   they reveal the secret of
that undying charm which modern literature can
never rival.   And just as experience of life and
human nature unfolds the meaning of the great
classic writers, so our moral and spiritual
experience opens up to us the meaning and
power of Scripture.   When we read the Bible at
first, it seems only an ancient book—picturesque,
it may be, and sublime, but without much vital
application.   Perhaps, like Narcissus, we gaze
at our own faces reflected on the surface of the

water. But when we have lived longer and
suffered awhile and undergone the temptations
and perplexities and bereavements of which the
Bible speaks, when we have been under the cloud
and passed through the sea, then these very
trials teach us to discern in Scripture depths
which we never saw before.

In one sense, indeed, the Bible is the simplest
of books, because it deals with elemental things
like birth and death and hunger and labour and
love and pain and parting, which go on in every
village every day. Such things seem commonplace, but they are the stuff out of which human
life is fashioned : and the aged come back to
brood over them and to feel that in these things
lie the real problems after all. But the Bible
is most profound, because it deals with the deep
original wound in human nature. It goes down
below the roots of man's misery and degradation
and remorse. It reveals the abysses of mercy
and judgment in which the foundations of
man's redemption are laid. " Deep calleth unto
deep " in the Book of God. Its friends are
exultations and agonies, and those impassioned
hours which interpret to us the passion of the
Gospel. The sciolists who declare that the well
is shallow are refuted by the common testimony
of the men who have drawn deepest from that
unfathomable, inexhaustible fountain. No one
else can claim to be a true expert in Holy Scripture. If the saints shall judge the world, then
surely it is the saints, and not the critics, who

shall judge the Bible. And this Book is compassed about with a great cloud of witnesses who cry with Augustine, *Mira profunditas, mi Deus, mira profunditas*.

Some one has said that everywhere in the Bible, if we dig deep enough, we find " Do right " at the bottom. Yet while this is true, it is far from being the total truth. For if we dig deeper still, we find each exhortation to right conduct based on the rock of the righteousness of God. While St. Paul lays down in detail the plain practical duties of daily life, he constantly grounds these duties on supernatural facts and enforces them by transcendent motives. For instance, in the Epistle to the Romans, when he has ended his mighty argument concerning the sovereign grace of God and uttered a doxology at its climax, the Apostle begins to draw the cords of Divine love closer round the conscience of the individual man. " I beseech you, *therefore*, brethren "—at the back of that word *therefore* lies the whole weight of Christian theology. Considering the wonder and glory of our election and redemption, what manner of persons ought we to be ? There is no other basis for ethics in the New Testament. The golden precepts of conduct given there depend upon heavenly sanctions and succours ; they are the rules for a redeemed life which is surrendered to the will of God. And so throughout the Bible, its doctrines and commands and promises open up vistas into the infinite. Its mystery is " the darkness of the pure, unsearchable sea."

We are familiar with the common phrases by which people label different schools of Christian thought and various types of religious character. We hear continually of the High Church and the Low Church and the Broad Church. Hutton wrote a memorable essay upon what he called the Hard Church. Now there is one type of experience which ought to characterize Christians whose spiritual life is fed from the well-spring of Holy Scripture. We may name it the Deep Church, because the hearts of its disciples are enlarged to apprehend the deep things of God. Those who muse and ponder over the profoundest thoughts of the Bible become more and more truly Deep Churchmen, as they are made partakers of the Divine nature and filled with the fullness of the Divine life.

BE OF GOOD CHEER

IN our familiar experience there are certain sayings and phrases which have become inextricably associated with some particular persons. It may be a father's favourite quotation, or a mother's pet proverb, or an old friend's characteristic little speech, racy of himself. If we chance to hear other people repeat them now, the syllables act like an incantation ; they call up the very voice and tone and smile which once

made those words homely music to our ears.
And beyond such individual memories, we
connect certain maxims with the men who
coined them and gave them currency. Often in
plays or novels some character is linked with a
phrase which becomes a kind of formula for
himself. And in history a great man's favourite
watchword comes to be stamped with his own
image and superscription ; it carries the salt
and savour of his personality. Men like Luther
and Cromwell and Nelson are instantly recalled
by the sayings attributed to them at critical
moments in their careers.

Now the same holds true, to some extent, even
in regard to our Lord and Master. One saying
of His, at any rate, must have been peculiarly
characteristic, because it clung so closely to the
memories of those who loved Him. This watchword we know was often on His lips, and always
in His heart—" Be of good cheer." On five
separate occasions we hear Christ using it to
comfort the forlorn children of men. And when
we consider a little, we understand how this
brief sentence could, in a manner, embody the
message of His life.

It was such a simple, homely thing to say.
Pascal has remarked how naturally Christ speaks
about eternal truths. " Be of good cheer "—
four little words in English, only two syllables in
Greek ; it is the very sentence we use when we
visit a friend in his sick chamber, or when we
meet a man who has had business losses or

family troubles. Often our " Cheer up ! "
means nothing more than vague goodwill ; when
we say it, we feel that we have, alas ! so little
warrant for our words. But when Jesus Christ
comes into the world saying " Be of good cheer,"
He speaks with absolute authority and perfect
knowledge and complete experience. For He
comes from the bosom of the Father, and He
is at home in the secrets of eternity. He has
sounded the awful abyss of evil, and wrestled
with all the hosts of darkness. This Man of
Sorrows gazes out upon the universe with eyes
full of quenchless courage, and there is victory
in the Voice which says " Be of good cheer."
It is His parting word to His friends when He
leaves them the night before His Passion—the
cry of a Conqueror, who can say already " It is
finished."

This was the very message which men most
needed. The age of the Advent was full of
profound and intense melancholy. " The drama
of ancient civilization was played out." Though
it might seem outwardly tranquil and prosperous, that first century was an age of iron and
not of gold—the saddest and most heartless age
of which history makes mention. The masters
of human wisdom were teaching doctrines of
despair. Into a corrupt and paralysed generation—in the fullness of time, which was also the
emptiness of time—God sent His Son to make
all things new. Christ came into a worn-out
world, bringing the energy of an endless life into

the midst of human impotence and despairing.
His was the Gospel of redemption and resurrection, of victory achieved and deliverance accomplished. No wonder its Author and Finisher
could bid men be of good cheer !

He is speaking the same supernatural promise
to His Church militant on earth to-day. And
we need it now, as men needed it long ago.
Strange analogies may be traced between the
first century and the twentieth. Men are still
tempted to become fatalists in politics and
pessimists in literature. There is the same
temptation to dull, faithless despondency, the
same weight of weariness and decadence as of
those on whom the ends of the world are come.
Even the bravest Christians grow daunted, not
merely by reason of failures in their own spiritual
experience, but more sadly still when Christ's
cause and kingdom seem to recede rather than
advance. But the Bible is full of God's
encouragements to the disappointed. Our Lord
is continually whispering to His disheartened
disciples, " Let not your heart be troubled,
neither let it be afraid." So may He grant us
His grace of good cheer day by day. May we
go about His work in that temper of grave,
sweet, unfaltering cheerfulness which is the very
spirit of Christ Himself. May we sing the
Te Deum until we forget the *De profundis*—
as Christians should. For the Christian faith
affirms that the most glorious things are true
already—true for us and for every man—and

that they never can be less than true. The
New Testament repeats and ratifies the cry of
the great Evangelical prophet : " Comfort ye,
comfort ye my people, saith your God."

THE WORDS OF THE LORD JESUS

Among the first Christians this seems to have
been a favourite watchword : *Remember the
words of the Lord Jesus, how He said* . . . By
true instinct those primitive disciples hung upon
the lips of their Lord and Master. They began
by being listeners, and they treasured up in their
hearts what they had heard the voice of Jesus
say. It is instructive to note that " obedience "
is derived from the same root as " audience."
The hearing ear and the willing heart are close
akin. The saints correspond to the angels in
this, that they do His commandments, hearken-
ing unto the voice of His word.

Christ's authentic sayings must have been
easy to remember. " One conspicuous fact in
the New Testament is the incomparable and
solitary relief in which they stand out by themselves." They bear a stamp and seal of their
own. As Deissmann puts it, they are seen to
be not separate pearls threaded on one string, but
flashes of one and the same diamond. The truth
and its Author are inseparable. Never man
spake like this Man. His words are so simple,
so translucent, and yet so penetrating, so full of

awful authority. He speaks with a tone and
accent which are not of this world. His voice
comes out of the bosom of the Father, and stirs
the echoes of eternity in our spirits as we listen.
To a Christian nothing sounds so conclusive
and final as the plain command, the explicit
promise of Jesus Christ. We understand that
strong assurance with which the Apostle could
quote : *He Himself hath said.* There is no
certainty for us like the *ipse dixit* of our
Redeemer.

Sometimes it appears to us strange that He
said so little, or rather that we have so little
of His own teaching left. All Christ's recorded
sayings put together fill but a narrow compass.
They could be easily printed in one issue of a
modern newspaper. Yet brief as they are, and
artless in outward form, His words changed the
axis of the world. And to-day as we brood over
them and try to understand them by obeying
them, we come to perceive more and more how
their limpid syllables are full of unfathomable
truth. It belongs to the power and wonder of
the words of the Lord Jesus that the holiest
Christian thinker can never exhaust them.
A wise man tells us that " life is spent in learning
the meaning of great words," and the sentence
is fulfilled for each believing student of the
sayings of Christ. In those familiar utterances
of His enshrined in the Gospels, which we all
know by rote, He has still many things to say
unto us, of which we have hardly an inkling

at present. He must have meant far more by
His words than we have ever grasped or guessed
hitherto.   Are there not points in His clearest
teaching which we pass over absently, listlessly ?
Are there not plain commands of His which we
listen to with a kind of bewilderment ?   We
cannot bear them.   We believe that our Lord
has spoken these hard, dark sayings, but we
cannot tell what He saith.

The Christian spends his life in learning how
much Christ's words really mean.   There are
gaps and blanks in the circle of our spiritual
knowledge, there are missing links in the chain
of our inner experience, without which we cannot
be made perfect.   The fatal thing is to fancy
that we have learned already all that Christ has
to teach us, that we have mastered the words
of the Lord Jesus.   The one thing needful for us
is to be humble and willing that these sayings
of His should master us more and more completely day by day.   For He is teaching His
disciples still, as surely as ever He taught them
in Galilee.   " All the words He ever spake,
still to us He speaketh."   And His messages,
like His mercies, are new every morning.
Through life's chequered experience the Spirit
of truth interprets and unfolds more and more
perfectly the words and the mind of Christ.

Let us remember, finally, that these sayings
are nothing but the self-expression of the
Speaker.   Our Lord's words are full of Himself,
because they proceed out of the abundance of

His heart. They are spirit and they are life,
and by them He still communicates Himself in
very deed and truth to as many as obey Him.
It was concerning such communion that Ignatius
wrote a deep mystical sentence :   " He that
hath the word of Jesus truly can hear His silence
also."

NOT AS THE WORLD GIVETH

WE are often exhorted to read the Bible just as
we would read any other book ; and on the face
of it this counsel is sound. For instance, the
correct text of Scripture has to be settled by the
same critical methods which are employed to
determine the text of other ancient writings.
Then we must take pains to obtain the best
possible translation of the text from the original
tongues. And, further, we must employ reason
as well as scholarship in order to understand
what is written. The great Reformers laid aside
the fantastic methods of interpretation which
had been dear to ecclesiastical students in earlier
ages, and maintained that the plain grammatical
meaning of any verse in the Bible must be taken
as conveying the primary intention of the writer.
The Churches of the Reformation made, and
still make, their appeal to the sense of Scripture
as determined by sound learning.

And yet when we have used all these resources
of intellect and education in order that we may

read the Bible just as we would read any other
book, we begin to discover that, after all, the
Bible is strangely unlike every other book in
existence. There resides in its pages one supreme characteristic which makes it to be the
Bible, and not a mere library of antique
Oriental literature. When Christian people
admire God's Book for its literary excellence, for
the eloquence or the poetry which it contains,
they are missing the mark. We degrade that
Book when we treat it as a collection of magnificent literature, almost as much as they do who
treat it as a primer of science or an almanac of
predictions. The message of the Bible has
nothing to do with things like these. The
kingdom of Scripture is not in word but in power.

When some secular man of letters turns over
the pages of the Old and New Testaments, he
may perhaps say to himself : " Here we have
a curious medley of Semitic legend and folklore,
fragments of ancient Hebrew history, some sublime poems and prophecies, all bound up with
the legal code of a primitive race. Then follow
the memoirs of a martyr, with certain missionary
travels and correspondence." Yet the literary
critic who sums up the Bible in this fashion has
entirely missed its distinctive and dominating
note. It never sets out to teach us the wisdom
of the world, or the wisdom of words. It confesses that it is a pilgrim and stranger upon earth.
When we study the broad drift and purport of
Scripture, we recognize running through it all one

unique feature—the gradual unveiling of the Divine character. The earlier portions reveal this overwhelming fact : that God is holy and that therefore man must be holy. And the final revelation of the Person of Jesus Christ sums up everything which went before it. All the words of God which were spoken of old in divers parts and in divers manners are so many fragments of the truth which forms a perfect whole in Christ. The more deeply we ponder the content of Holy Scripture, the more surely are we convinced that never book spake like this Book : for we realize that it is nothing less than the sacrament of Redeeming Love.

There are many avenues along which the Bible comes home to us in a different way from any other literature in the world. Modern reviewers are fond of telling us, for instance, that before we can appreciate any great book or grasp its meaning, we must first of all sympathize with the idea and intention which inspired it ; we must read it from its author's point of view. So also, before we can appreciate and understand the Scriptures, we must come into harmony with God's will, we must be informed and possessed by His Spirit, we must sympathize with His purpose for mankind. And concerning this Book we may say that the Author is never absent or out of reach : He will have us converse with Him and inquire of Him even while we read.

Again, it comes true concerning the gifts of this world, that they seem most golden when

we first receive them. In course of time they
turn stale with keeping, they grow threadbare
with use. Whereas the best wine of the Bible
always seems reserved until the last. Its revelation remains unexhausted and inexhaustible.
Has not the New Testament still many things to
say unto us, as we are able to bear them ?
Why, we have never yet fathomed some of its
simplest words about elementary Christian
duties—about the virtue of absolute forbearance,
of utterly forgiving our enemies, about the
irresistible might of peacefulness, about the
deadly danger of riches, about the beatitude of
literal simplicity and poverty. The Church
has not outgrown the Gospels. Often we find
that an old man has lost interest in the literature
which entranced him once, when he was a boy.
But at the end of the day, as the shadows
lengthen, the Bible becomes more and more
wonderful to those who have loved it longest,
who know it best. Amid all the disappointments
and disillusions of this world we may still hear
it whisper : " Not as the world giveth give I unto
you."

THE SIGN OF THE CROSS

It is difficult for us to realize that throughout
the ancient Roman world the word " cross "
had the same horrible associations which surround our word " gibbet." It was the instru-

ment of a shameful and lingering death, which
was reserved for criminals and slaves. It meant
all, and more than all, that the gallows and the
guillotine mean now. Can we imagine a new
religious movement adopting the hangman's
halter for its badge and blazon ? And yet nothing less than this actually happened. Jesus
Christ redeemed the very cross on which He was
crucified, so that it has become the supreme
token of His eternal sacrifice, which embodies
the agony and victory of Divine Love. Beyond
any other symbol it sums up the heart and
essence of our holy faith. We see the cross
surmounting the spires and domes of Christendom. Nay, almost every Gothic church and
cathedral is built on a cruciform foundation,
and has the cross for its very ground-plan.
Even unbelievers and persecutors still recognize
this sign as the characteristic emblem of all
that Christians believe and adore. During the
Boxer outbreak in China, when anyone was
captured and suspected of being a convert,
it was a common thing for the Boxers to trace
a cross in the dust and then to order their
prisoner to trample on it. Hundreds of humble
Chinese Christians accepted martyrdom rather
than commit that act of apostasy ; for to trample on the cross was openly to deny their
Redeemer.

In primitive times the sign of the cross may
have been used by scattered disciples as a token
by which they could recognize one another amid

their heathen surroundings, perhaps in the same sort of way as Freemasons recognize each other by signs. Among the Churches of the Reformation the practice of crossing oneself was generally abandoned, on account of the superstitions which had grown up and clustered round that habit. The cross was degraded into a fetish and employed as a magic spell. And there are regions in Europe to-day where the most depraved persons always cross themselves religiously before they commit some act of special wickedness. Such profanity warns us that even a sacred sign can be divorced from its moral and spiritual meaning, and reminds us that all signs and forms may become worse than useless except so far as they are the sincere expression of faith and character.

In Canada an Italian immigrant objected that there was no cross stamped on the cover of an Italian Bible which was offered him. " No," replied the colporteur, " but if you read the book, you will find the cross inside." The deep truth of his answer may appear from an illustration. Perhaps the noblest summary of the Gospel familiar to English ears has been given in Handel's *Messiah*. That wonderful work belongs to no special Church. Every syllable of its language is taken from the Bible. And it pierces and subdues us all not simply by its matchless music, but chiefly because this music recites the whole drama of our redemption from its earliest promise on to its final climax and

triumph. It we were to blot out from the
Messiah every bar of what can be called Passion
Music, if we cancelled every word and note which
sing of Christ crucified, we might judge from
what remained how indelibly revelation is
marked with the sign of the cross.

The dimensions of the cross—its length and
breadth and height and depth—surpass man's
measurement. The pages of the New Testament point towards a Divine mystery which lies
beyond all our explaining and understanding.
God's eternal act of reparation and retrieval is
mightier than any human theory of atonement.
To all generations the cross stands as a sign
rather than a definition. Yet here, as nowhere
else, we discern the very signature of faith ;
we recognize the hall-mark of the faithful.

One most certain test of our Christianity must
be whether we carry in our own habits and
characters any corresponding seal. Those individuals and institutions which are set apart for
Christian service must surely be marked with the
sign of the cross. And the tokens of the true
cross in our lives are precisely those acts and
decisions of ours which transfix our common
selfishness. Whenever we deny ourselves
willingly for the sake of others who do not love
us, whenever we spend pains and patience to
understand those who have no sympathy with
us, whenever we give up ease or profit or
reputation for the unthankful and the evil, we
are beginning to receive the sacred marks of

likeness to the Crucified. His call still says, "If any man will come after Me, let him deny himself." And nothing carries real spiritual potency and fruitfulness except sacrifice. Some of our great public charities are carried on without costing anyone much serious self-denial; they are maintained out of superfluities—and so they fail and grow mechanical because they lack the mysterious virtue which only personal sacrifice communicates. On the other hand, the sign of the cross is the death-blow to self-aggrandisement and self-advertisement and self-display. The most absolute devotion will not strive or cry or lift up its voice in the streets. It is content to go hidden and unrecognized among men. But if we could search into the secrets of a saintly character, we should always find that the cross itself is there.

THE SALT OF THE EARTH

To appreciate the force of the references to salt in the Gospels, we must recollect that towns by the Lake of Galilee carried on an important local trade of fish-curing in New Testament times. Writers like Strabo show us that the pickled fish exported from the Lake had spread its fame throughout the Roman world. And we can hardly doubt that this familiar industry prompted, or at least pointed, our Lord's allusions to salt. For any place where fish are caught and cured must store salt in considerable quantities. Moreover, the Lake of Galilee is a torrid basin, which lies nearly 700 feet below the level of the Mediterranean. On those shores no fish could possibly be kept fresh for many hours after it was landed : it must be cooked or cured promptly. Again, fishermen's luck is everywhere a proverb of fluctuation. In the Gospels we read how nets were cast fruitlessly all night long and then grew heavy on a sudden with an immense haul, which had to be taken off at once to the curing-house, or salted down provisionally till it could be transported there. Years ago it was my fortune to sail on board a North Sea herring lugger which carried barrels of coarse salt to preserve any fish that we could not bring fresh into market ; and I have heard bitter complaints among the crew when the salt was found to be of bad quality. It seems certain that the fishermen of Galilee were as familiar with salting as with fishing—although the latter was their proper work. They would understand their Master whether He called them "fishers of men" or "salters of men." They would appreciate His meaning when He spoke of refuse salt in wholesale fashion as "cast out and trodden under foot of men." How naturally the command fell upon their ears, "Have salt among yourselves" ! How forcibly sounded the homely similitude, "Ye are the salt of the earth" !

In every country salt stands for what gives

flavour to food and preserves it against putre-
faction. A gifted modern Englishman has
praised the virtues of light and sweetness ; but
there was an old Roman proverb to the effect
that " nothing does more good than sunshine
and salt." In His analogy our Lord lays stress
upon that special quality in Christian character
which forms an antiseptic to the corruption
which is in the world. It has been said that the
vice which Christ could least tolerate was the vice
of insipidity. Assuredly the man after His own
heart is the man whose goodness is not negative
but positive, the man who exerts an energetic
moral reaction upon every evil which he meets,
the man who is not only a protest against all
things foul and false but a living power that
makes for purity.

A genuine Christian cannot fail to arrest and
even antagonize other men by his solemn sense
of things unseen and eternal, by his passionate
spirit of brotherhood, by his unquenchable
hatred of tyranny and wrong. He must needs
be a standing witness to other men that " the
lust of the flesh and the lust of the eyes and the
pride of life are not of the Father but of the
world." Richard Baxter used to say that it is
because we have so few high saints that we have
so many low sinners. And we must confess
sorrowfully that those disciples who are indeed
the salt of the earth have never been plentiful.
Nevertheless the Church endures and overcomes
by virtue of living examples like theirs. And

probably " there has scarcely been a town in any
Christian country since the time of Christ where
a century has passed without exhibiting a
character of such elevation that his mere
presence has shamed the bad and made the good
better, and has been felt at times like the
presence of God Himself."

Finally, we recognize a real sense in which the
Bible itself deserves to be described as the salt
of the earth. In any country where God's Book
has become a household volume there cannot but
exist a loftier ethical standard, a purer atmosphere, a clearer vision of the great White Throne.
Scripture is instinct with a power for righteousness, which penetrates and informs and judges
the character of a nation. That moral seriousness which has characterized so much of the best
English literature is due to the fact that in
England the people are acquainted with Holy
Writ. We may quote the words of the late
venerable Archbishop Alexander uttered from
the pulpit of Westminster Abbey : " The
presence of the Book of God in any land, far
and wide, gives at least a hush of awe and the
sanctity of a great ideal—so that when a certain
point of corruption has been reached the whole
community cries out indignantly at last, ' We
have read Christ's Word. Christ's voice is upon
the air. No more of this ! ' " Assuredly, salt is
good.

IN WHOSE HEART ARE
THE HIGHWAYS TO ZION

WHEN I go back to the dawn of consciousness and try to recall the things which have left deepest marks in memory, I always think of certain green paths across the meadows, where I played and picked cowslips as a child. The faces of the other children who played there have grown misty, but the old familiar footpaths are ineffaceable. They belong to those first affections, those earliest recollections, which cling round the roots of human nature.

The grand road from the mountain goes shining to the sea,
    And there is traffic on it, and many a horse and cart,
But the little roads of Cloonagh are dearer far to me,
    And the little roads of Cloonagh go rambling through my heart.

Antiquarians tell us that the oldest roads in England had been worn by men's feet for centuries before the Roman conquest. Here and there these ancient roads survive in hollow tracks which hide themselves under the ridges of the moorland and creep into the recesses of the hills, so that a primitive traveller could pass on his way secure from observation. Such tracks are an allegory of that which lies embedded in the secret places of the soul. And there is a sense in which this saying of the Psalmist may be taken as referring not merely to elect individuals, but to the human race : "A wanderer is man from his birth." He pitches his tent under strange stars, and ventures across uncharted seas in quest of visionary treasure. But sooner or later—it may be amid a brawling market-place, it may be alone in some great and terrible wilderness—he is smitten down by his own desolation and misery; and then an inward voice wakes up and whispers, " I will arise and go to my Father." For the way that leads home lies in the deep recesses of his heart.

Again, we may surely apply these words in a true sense to describe the Bible itself. Many have stumbled at Holy Scripture, because outwardly it is so unlike what they would have imagined and expected God's revelation to be. They feel that it has so little unity or symmetry. In their eyes the Book appears only a collection of fragments of ancient literature—poems and prophecies and chronicles and correspondence. But Scripture after all exists for one severely practical purpose, and outside that purpose it has little use or meaning. The Bible is the Bible, because it is able to make us wise unto salvation, even though it leave us ignorant about everything else besides. Here is the kernel and essence of the whole matter, compared with which no minor questions deserve consideration. We can say of this Book, as of no other, that in its heart are the highways to Zion—along which we travel to the sky.

Now a highway exists not to be talked about, but to be travelled on. We can only know it properly by walking along it, and it serves no real end except as it is put to this practical use.

In a Korean village there was a Christian convert who learned the whole of the Sermon on the Mount by heart, and then he set out and tramped a hundred miles that he might recite it to his pastor. When he had finished the recital, he was told that he must now put the Sermon into practice. His reply was, " But that is the way in which I managed to learn it. At first I tried to commit it to memory by rote, and it would not stick. So I hit upon this plan : I would learn a verse, and then go out and find a heathen neighbour and practise that verse on him. Then I found that it would stick ! "

The Old Testament contains one immortal picture which illustrates the wistful, eager faith conveyed in these words. It shows us the young Hebrew exile at the court of Babylon, who had courage to open his lattice at sunrise and noon and sunset, so that he might pray looking out across the desert towards the Holy City. He was not afraid of the king's commandment ; in his heart were the highways to Zion.

How shall we recognize the true pilgrim ? We may know him—but not by his outward habit and vesture, not " by his cockle hat and staff and his sandal shoon." The decisive test goes deeper, and tries the attitude of the inward man. Has he learned the Divine secret of detachment ? Does he dare to " let the world go and take love " ? Does he carry in his heart the wisdom of Egypt, or the market-places of Babylon, or the highways to Zion ? For this is the token of those who are indeed pilgrims of eternity. They desire a better country, that is an heavenly. They look not at the things that are seen, but at the things that are not seen ; for the things that are seen are temporal, but the things that are not seen are eternal. In the cloisters at Canterbury there is an epitaph cut in the stone over Dean Alford's grave, which a Christian might well write over the doorway of the office where he works and of the chamber where he lies down to sleep. The words are : *Diversorium viatoris Hierosolymam proficiscentis*—the inn of a traveller on his way to Jerusalem.

LET PATIENCE HAVE HER PERFECT WORK

THIS homely virtue of patience becomes a kind of password in the New Testament. And when we consider, we can see how there was peculiar need for such a virtue in the primitive Church. Christ's earliest disciples had not the sanction of long Christian centuries behind them, as we have. In a sense they were explorers and discoverers ; they were framing the spiritual alphabet by means of which we learn to read. They were making a supreme experiment ; and in all experiments men have need of patience, lest they lose heart too soon. Then again, the first believers had not only much to discover which we inherit, but much also to endure which we escape. That was a time when all who would live godly in Christ Jesus must suffer persecution and resist even unto blood, striving against sin. Assuredly those confessors of the creed of martyrdom had need of patience. Moreover, the early Christians were penetrated and possessed with one unspeakable expectation. They endured in hope of their Lord's return. They trusted that they should not taste of death until they had seen His kingdom come with power. Wistfully and patiently they watched in the face of His delay. " O tarry thou the Lord's leisure " was the apostolic message, as year after year slipped by and the Advent hope burned dim. " Rest in the Lord, and wait patiently for Him. Fret not thyself in any wise . . ." The ancient Psalm must have come home to them with vivid and pathetic power.

Yet the same exhortation applies to us twentieth-century Christians, on whom the ends of the age are come. In these last days men grow more than ever restless for change, and fitful in temper, and hasty in experiment, and hungry for quick returns. Even in the Church have not the strength and glory somehow faded out of our Christian ideal of patience ? Englishmen naturally admire doggedness and tenacity of temper. They boast that they never know when they are beaten. But they commonly think of patience as a passive quality, suitable for women and for invalids. They recall patient Enid and patient Griselda ; but in their hearts they hardly rank this virtue among the highest attributes of manhood. Our wisest English teachers warn us against such a mistake. John Bunyan understood better : in his Interpreter's House, Patience appears as the deep, steady, self-controlled character, in contrast with shallow, sensual levity which grasps the present and misses the future. In Spenser's *Faerie Queene* we find Patience figured as a manly virtue, and placed as physician in the House of Holiness, to typify the healing power of long-suffering love. On the other hand, Spenser depicts Impatience as one of the hags who attend the evil spirit of Passion, Impotence being the other. And in practical life do we not find that impatience and impotence go hand in hand ? The wilful, hasty spirit always leads on to weakness and failure. Whereas nothing on earth is so invincible as patience—the " equal temper of heroic hearts, to strive, to seek, to find, and not to yield."

Patience is really the test and token of inward strength. St. Paul prays for his friends at Colossæ that they may be strengthened with power according to the might of God's glory— *unto all patience.* Only a soul thus strengthened can toil on, undaunted and serene in the teeth of trial and disappointment. For apart from patience, faith herself does not inherit the promises. The victory which overcometh the world is won by invincible, irresistible patience. We learn in the end that we can best " conquer pain by suffering, and want by wanting, and loss by losing, and failure by failing, and death itself by dying."

Amid the manifold discouragements and disappointments involved in all genuine Christian service, one chief secret of endurance lies in considering Him who endured such contradiction of sinners against Himself, lest we grow weary and faint in our minds. To be misunderstood and misrepresented and maligned ; to be hindered and thwarted by the very people you are most anxious to befriend ; to be deceived by those you trust and betrayed by those you love— these are experiences which no faithful Christian worker can altogether escape. Nay, sometimes the contradiction of sinners seems less harassing than the contradiction of saints—the criticism and contempt which you meet with at the hands of religious people because you follow not with them. The servants of Jesus Christ need a double share of His own patience, that they may overcome this evil with good.

" The signs of an apostle were wrought among you," says St. Paul, " in all patience, by wonders and mighty works." And here is the mightiest work, and the greatest wonder of all. To make the best possible of each one of our fellow-workers, to put up with the froward, to make allowance for the foolish, to submit to having our judgment overruled, not even to claim our own rights or to assert our own position, to endure all things from all men even when they try our patience **most**—here is one great unexplored secret of Christian success.

Each of Christ's commandments has its roots in a corresponding promise. We must let patience have her perfect work in us, because patience belongs to the perfectness of God. Nothing in the whole experience of the spiritual life is so moving, so marvellous, as our Lord's infinite forbearance in His dealings with His disciples. Year after year He bears with us in His inexhaustible, incredible patience—which is never wearied and never spent, which grows stronger as our claim on it grows weaker, which triumphs even over our abuse of it, which sees of its travail and is satisfied at last.

God's inexpressible patience with us inspires us to be patient towards Him. When we remember how He bears all things from us and hopes all things concerning us, can we not go on bearing anything that He sends and doing anything that He requires, without asking why ? Since He never gives us up, or despairs of us, or deserts us, how can we give Him up, or despair of Him, or desert Him ? Nothing but patience can have a perfect work in the soul. But faith in the God of all patience teaches us to say, " The Lord shall perfect that which concerneth me. Thy mercy, O Lord, endureth for ever. Forsake not the work of Thine own hands."

AT the end of nineteen centuries Christians find it hard to realize how miraculous was the original novelty of the Gospel. The law and the prophets had indeed prepared a way for it among holy men of old ; yet it came upon mankind as literally Good News of God. It made a fresh beginning, which broke through the ancient routine of time. Through unnumbered ages summer and winter, seed-time and harvest, had gone on in unchanging succession, and empires had risen and fallen again, and faiths and philosophies had appeared and had their vogue and then perished and passed away—so that cynics went about declaring, " That which hath been shall be, and there is no new thing under the sun." Against the bondage of this iron chain of sequence, the soul cries out for liberty to believe in God as the Eternal Beginner. And at last men heard the Good News that verily He had visited and redeemed His people. The advent of Jesus Christ was the coming in of a fresh spiritual order, so that " we can only compare it with the first day of creation or the last day of the world." The Love of God Himself entered this dark earth in the sacred year from which we have learnt to date all our history. Pagan peoples had eras of their own. The Romans counted time from the year of the foundation of their city. The Jews went back to the year when, as they thought, the world had

been made.   But all the calendars of Christendom reckon from the coming of Him Who
is Himself the Beginning of the creation of God.

The Gospel is full of promises of new begin-
nings.   It breathes abroad like morning air, and
tells us of a new birth, a new name, a new song.
Its charter is called the New Testament.   Its
great watchwords are resurrection and regenera-
tion.   Christ announces something far more
radical than any scheme for social betterment—
something far deeper and more difficult.   He
undertakes the conversion of human nature and
human character.   Christ proclaims that He can
make base men holy, and proud men humble,
and selfish men generous.   He proposes to trans-
form sinners into saints.   The Gospel comes to
each separate sinner, however hardened and degraded, with the amazing promise that even he
in his own experience may start afresh with the
heart of a little child, and walk henceforth in
newness of life, through the mercy and grace and
power of God.

The Christian Church can never afford to
forget its revolutionary function.   It exists to
bring about spiritual conversions, to make all
things new for the blackest and basest souls,
to seek and to save the lost.   In our pursuit of
general philanthropies, excellent and necessary
as they are, we are often tempted to lose sight
of this supreme object.   Again and again the
Church has waxed cold in love, and been content
merely to mitigate misery and diffuse enlighten-

ment. But Christianity sacrifices its very soul when it abandons its missionary character and despairs of the conversion of sinners, when it becomes no more than an institution for improvement or a machine for social reform. " When the power of reclaiming the lost dies out of the Church, it ceases to be the Church. . . . But while that power remains, there, whatever is wanting, it may still be said that the tabernacle of God is with men."

Behold, I make all things new. This same mighty promise holds good for each individual Christian along the whole course of his pilgrimage. For it is the essence of that pilgrimage that it must be a progress. To follow Christ can never mean to live by mere convention or to settle down into the ruts of religious routine. Nothing is so fatal to the soul as a stagnant experience. No believer can exist upon the remainder biscuit of his own spiritual past. We must gather our manna fresh, morning by morning. Every day God has prepared for His children some better thing than they tasted the day before. Each new year ought to bring us new discoveries of the unsearchable riches of Christ. What Christian has ever exhausted the Bible ? Holy Scripture continually unfolds fresh depths of meaning to those who read it in the faith of the pilgrims, that " the Lord has yet more light and truth to break forth from His Word."

To-day, the ancient promise to make all things

new is being fulfilled in strange and terrible
fashion before our eyes. No man living can
remember the sky so thick with tokens of
tremendous change. The world is seething and
fermenting with new ideas and hopes, rushing
into new experiments, exulting in new opportunities. Our newspapers read like comments
upon the text : " Now that which decayeth
and waxeth old is ready to vanish away." Yet
faithful Christians can lift up their heads and
rejoice, in the confidence that He who is the
Eternal Regenerator and Reconstructor sitteth
on the throne, ruling over our mortal tribulations
and confusions. For each man, and for each
nation, the Lord is still making all things new.
In this season of incalculable transformation,
we can take heart to believe in a moral and
spiritual advance beyond all that the Church
has dared to hope for. Amid the swift un-
foldings of such days as ours, it seems as though
anything might happen before this generation
passes away. There may be some standing here
who shall not taste of death until they see the
kingdom of God come with power.

O TASTE AND SEE

IN this world of shadows we find many things
which are difficult enough to think out satisfac-
torily or to explain in words ; yet they become
simple enough when we take them away from

theory and test them by practical experience. Consider, for instance, a common bicycle. If a man sets out to inquire scientifically how a bicycle moves and balances, he soon gets entangled among problems in higher dynamics. But when he leaves off asking curious questions and sets himself to learn to ride, he quickly proves that a bicycle's motion is possible and easy and pleasant. Now, in the same sort of way, not a few religious problems are extremely perplexing theoretically. There is, for example, the endless puzzle in philosophy, how God's foreknowledge can co-exist with man's free-will. Or, again, there is the mysterious question in theology, how Christ's death avails to bring about the pardon of human guilt. We may speculate and argue and wrangle for years without coming nearer to an intellectual explanation. Yet these profound problems solve themselves in the experience of humble Christians. As we give ourselves up to do the will of God, we discover that there is no conflict between Divine grace and human liberty. As we repent and forsake our selfishness, we prove that the forgiveness of sins is a glorious reality, even though we have no skill to explain how our forgiveness was purchased. Concerning such a spiritual problem as atonement or election, we may say reverently, *solvitur ambulando*.

The truth is, no man can grasp Christian theory except in so far as he translates it into Christian practice. Doubts and difficulties are

not cured by brooding over them and debating
them ;   but we can resolve them by patient
obedience to what we know already of the will of
God.   Religion is not a Divine science but a
Divine life.   The Gospel of Christ cannot
possibly be understood and appreciated except
in terms of experience.   It is like the ancient
Greek Mysteries at Eleusis, whose secrets were
hidden from profane persons outside the gates.
You had to become a neophyte yourself and submit to the training and preparation and then
cross the threshold of the shrine, before you could
guess the privileges of the initiates within.   Even
so to master the mysteries of the kingdom of
heaven you must stoop to enter it as a little
child.   For God hides His secrets from the wise
and prudent and reveals them unto babes.

In religion, an ounce of personal experience is
worth a ton of borrowed theology.   As an old
writer says :   " God is best discerned by a spiritual touch.   We must see with our own eyes and
hear with our own ears, and our own hands must
handle the word of life.   For the soul has its
senses as well as the body.   And therefore the
Psalmist, when he would teach us how to know
the Divine goodness, calls not for speculation,
but for sensation, saying, not ' O argue and
understand ! ' but ' O taste and see how
gracious the Lord is ! ' "

Since the Christian religion is above all things
an experience, it follows that no one is qualified
to become its critic who is not first of all its

expert. What can be more futile than to discuss and argue and analyse, while we go on refusing to taste ? The time for criticism comes when the new wine has passed the lips—and lo ! it makes them that are asleep to speak and the tongue of the dumb to sing. We are not fit to form a proper estimate in regard to Christ till we have first tasted of His cup.

This same principle moreover applies also in a measure to criticism of the Scriptures. Nothing is easier than to ask unanswerable questions about the Bible ; nothing is cheaper than to condemn it for not being what it never pretends to be, for not explaining what it never sets out to reveal. We shall always miss our way in this Book until we try to approach it from its own point of view. Most of the difficulties which men discover in the New Testament are quite irrelevant to its real purpose—which is to reveal the glory of God in the face of Jesus Christ and to bring our spirits into immediate contact with His everlasting Love. The sure way to appreciate the Scriptures is to begin by leaving on one side those books and chapters which seem dark and perplexing, and to concentrate our attention on the things concerning Christ Himself, until our hearts receive some beams and rays from that Countenance which is brighter than the sun. The critic of the New Testament must be, first of all, its expert. And even then, when he tries to explain to others what he himself has learnt and known, his best words must sound ineffectual. What is the use of speaking to people in a language of which they have never learnt the vocabulary or practised the grammar ? The one thing left to say is this : " *O taste and see!* Taste for yourself, learn for yourself, see for yourself, how gracious the Lord is. Trust for yourself, and prove how blessed is the man that trusteth in Him."

IF IT WERE NOT SO

THE Bible has a reserve and reticence of its own. It tells us much, but it leaves much unspoken and unexplained. The substance of revelation is nothing less than the character of God, and Holy Scripture contains the one life-giving record of His purpose and His love for men. Yet the glory of the Gospel is compassed about with clouds and darkness. A little child will often ask questions about the redemption of the world to which the wisest saint can give no answers at all. Doubtless in this life it is part of our education to walk by faith and not by sight. Moreover, it seems that human souls on earth are incapable of enduring the full splendour of Light which has no shadows. So, when we come to Christ with our perplexed and importunate questionings, He quiets us with His compassionate word : " I have yet many things to say unto you, but ye cannot bear them now."

Nevertheless, on certain points we may

venture to draw inferences from the very silence of Scripture, a silence which is sometimes not less eloquent than speech. There are elemental truths which the Gospel simply takes for granted. In His own teaching our Lord hardly stops to affirm explicitly either that men are sinful or that men are immortal. His words are always based on these two great presuppositions—both of them alien to many modern thinkers. The New Testament sets out with the assumption that every man's first and bitterest need is his need to be forgiven, and that every man must enter upon the life of the world to come.

The same principle holds true in regard to the promises of God. In the pages of Scripture are given unto us exceeding great and precious promises, which have been verified in the experience of the faithful. Yet there remain other promises which God has written in books not made with hands, promises which are wrapped up in the frame and nature of things, promises which are implied rather than in so many words expressed. For what constitutes the value and preciousness of any Divine promise ? It is precious as a token of God's mind and heart towards His children, as a revelation of the nature of the Most High. Now every revelation which we can receive of our Creator involves in itself some revelation concerning His creatures as well, just as the earth is affected by every virtue and potency in the sun. As I watched the sunset one evening, a

5

large sun-spot was clearly visible, lying like a
withered leaf on the red disk. Next morning
most of the papers appeared without telegrams,
because a magnetic storm had hindered the
transmission of messages over the wires. And
these two facts—the celestial and the terrestrial,
the sun-spot and the storm—were closely con-
nected, though we cannot precisely explain how.
Similarly every fact about God must involve
exceeding great and precious consequences for
man. Indeed, the written and explicit promises
of Scripture are precious because they express
the Divine nature. A promise is a means to an
end. Its office is to lead us up beyond itself to
the Eternal Love. Believers who begin by
clinging closely to chapter and verse learn the
profounder truth of God's unspoken and unspeakable fidelity. They rest upon God Himself. They ask, as children might ask, " Is it
like Him ? " They win the beatitude of those
who have not seen and yet have believed.

Consider some consequences of this spiritual
principle. Often we hear God's promises set in
contrast to His commandments. And yet every
commandment really implies in itself a corresponding promise. Our Lord never lays on His
disciples a burden altogether beyond their
strength. He knows our frame : He is touched
with the feeling of our infirmities. He is no
austere task-master to mock us with impossible
orders. He cannot tantalize us with ideals
hopelessly and for ever out of our reach. When

Christ said to the cripple "Arise and walk," it is written "Immediately his feet and ankle-bones received strength." So each one of God's commands to us must needs carry with it the potency of its own fulfilment. Such a command is really a promise read backwards—a promise, as it were, in disguise.

This holds true also of the law graven on man's heart. Each whisper of conscience, each claim of loyalty, each prompting of tenderness, is also a promise that we are able to obey it if we will. If you take a torn, soiled bank-note and hold it up to the light, you can read woven into the paper the water-mark of its value. So even in the very pattern and texture of man's nature we can read something of its "whence" and its "whither," we can trace the imprint of its worth, the faded promise of its destiny. The earnest expectation of the creature waits for the manifestation of the sons of God. Every other created being finds somewhere an environment adapted to its needs. Desire in nature is the forerunner and prophecy of satisfaction. Each migratory instinct meets a climate to match it at last. So even our sense of limitation and insufficiency is a promise of some better thing. Our shame and horror of evil are a promise that we were created for purity. Our hunger and thirst after righteousness are a promise of robes to be one day washed white. Why is man's heart fashioned so that he knows himself to be a stranger and a pilgrim upon earth, encamped here but not domesticated, like autumn swallows ready to take wing for summer beyond the sea ? Experiences like these—and they are the deepest realities of our being—carry with them an exceeding great and precious promise. In our Father's house are many mansions : *if it were not so*, He would have told us.

The same principle holds good also with regard to the common instincts, the collective hopes, of the Christian Church. The ancient legend of the founding of Rome told how the eagles promised empire to a lonely watcher on the Aventine. Our Lord Himself persistently promised empire to His apostles. From the beginning He has inspired His Church with an imperial instinct for world-wide expansion and conquest. The missionary impulse of the Gospel belongs to the very nature of redemption itself. What Christ has done for us cannot be for us only ; it must concern every man : and so our Christian faith carries the great implicit assurance that it shall become the common possession of mankind at last.

IN THE LIGHT OF THE WAR

THERE were two books, and only two books, which Christ required men to read. One was the Scripture. Our Lord Himself habitually took the Old Testament for granted. He appealed to it, and argued from it, and opened it to His disciples, and asked in surprise, " Have ye never read ? " Yet, so far as we know, He never encouraged them to study commentaries. The Jewish rabbis had overlaid the text of Scripture with an elaborate embroidery of interpretation. But Christ had no love for these rabbinic notes and glosses. He condemned the scribes for making the Word of God of none effect by their tradition—darkening its meaning and explaining its commandments away. There are still Christians who forget that the power of the Bible does not reside in the books which men have written about it. Holy Scripture must always be its own best commentary. The proper introduction to the New Testament is contained in the Old, just as the final explanation of the Old Testament is supplied by the New. Probably the best notes and comments on the Bible are derived from the collective experience of those saints who have obtained its promises and have entered into its rest. In this sense few Christians would deny that the Church serves as the standing interpreter of the Scriptures. While above and beyond these, penetrating and informing them all, the same Holy Spirit Who spake by holy men of old still inspires and instructs the humblest reader who seeks His aid in studying His message. Concerning the Bible, we may say : " God is His own interpreter, and He will make it plain."

Besides the Bible, there was one other volume which Christ required men to read—the book of Providence, in which new pages are still being written by the Divine finger. Not once nor twice our Lord asked : " Can ye not discern the signs of the times ? " The things that were actually happening in the world appeared to Him like a commentary on Scripture. To His eyes present events were all instinct with God's purpose and working out God's will, and so they illustrated and confirmed God's revelation. Christ was continually saying to His disciples, " This day is this Scripture fulfilled in your ears." The ancient prophecies were always coming true, the ancient promises and warnings were constantly being fulfilled. And if we have faith in the living God we shall still discern God's purpose moving in human affairs, God's judgment accomplished in spite of conflict and confusion, God's will working even amid the woe and anguish which have fallen upon the world.

Have we not discovered that the war has been writing a new commentary on the Bible ? During these last years we have begun to read God's Book with larger, other eyes. Much of it was composed originally amid great tribulation ; and in our present tribulation it speaks to our hearts with a strange and piercing power which it never had before. Familiar words of Scripture come home to us with new meaning. Truths which had faded and been forgotten shine out with fresh light. In peace-time we shut our eyes to the fact that the Bible is so full of fighting. We passed over passages like the solemn vision

of the Apocalypse, which shows us the armies
that are in heaven riding after their Captain :
He is clothed with a vesture dipped in blood, and
in righteousness He doth judge and make war.
Whatever these awful symbols stand for, they
mean far more to us to-day than they used to
mean in times of peace.

Now that many men have been learning for the
first time in their lives how to spell patriotism,
we realize how much of the Scripture was
written by red-hot patriots. In captivity and
exile they longed for their native land. By
the waters of Babylon they wept as they remembered Zion ; they might almost be modern
prisoners of war interned in a hostile country.

Again, we have come to realize how much of
the Bible stands out against a crimson background of atrocity and massacre. Ancient
tyrants like Pharaoh and Sennacherib and
Nebuchadnezzar ravaged and slaughtered and
enslaved without pity. It was during the
horrors of the Indian Mutiny that British officers
wrote home to England and confessed that now
for the first time they had some insight into the
meaning of the imprecatory Psalms. Men who
fought in the Great War have seen things
which make them confess as much to-day.

In our prosperous years of peace multitudes of
Christians had left off believing in the existence
of the devil. They quietly ignored the teaching
of the New Testament, which does not explain
Satan, but always takes him for granted as a

dreadful reality. But we have been forced back into the attitude of the apostles and evangelists. To-day Christians everywhere are driven to believe that there is a devil, because they have come face to face with so much naked devilry.

To many of us the war has brought the Bible home to our hearts more closely still, making the solemn phrases of Scripture glow and burn with significance. " God gave His only Son " : so many fathers and mothers have given their sons ! And those lads, who willingly went in jeopardy of their lives for the sake of others, themselves entered into the very soul and secret of the Gospel. We talk and theorize about sacrifice, but they understand the solemn reality. Think of the multitudes of the wounded, the crippled, the shattered. As we met them in their hospital uniforms, we could only repeat to ourselves the echoes of sacred words : " . . . They have come out of the great tribulation. . . . Greater love hath no man than this." It is when we catch the high, heroic passion of those who count not their lives dear unto them, the spirit of the crusader and the martyr, it is then, and not till then, that the New Testament begins to unfold to us its inner meaning. The war has been a commentary on the Bible.

Finally, Scripture is full of dark, mysterious words concerning the great and terrible day of the Lord—a day of fiery trial for all men on earth, a day of testing and decision, a day when foulness and falsehood and cruelty shall be judged and doomed, a day when humility and pureness and truth shall come to their own at last. *The trumpet shall sound*—what man is so deaf that he has not heard it pealing ? *The powers that are in heaven shall be shaken*—what man is so blind that he cannot see them tottering to their fall ? Have we faith to lift up our heads, because our redemption draweth nigh ? Are we proud and thankful that God has counted us worthy to endure this ordeal, to share its dangers and its sacrifices, to prove that there are things far more precious than money, things far dearer than life ? This is indeed the day of the Lord, a day of revelation and resurrection, a day when the Bible is more alive than ever and means more than ever. For the heart of man is still young, and the Spirit of God has not died out.

THE FIELD IS THE WORLD

THE Charter of Christian Missions stands written in the parting commandment of Jesus Christ to His disciples. His final commission is recorded in each of the Gospels, and in the Acts as well. No other precept of our Lord comes to us with the same five-fold attestation. When we feel defeated or disheartened, we simply fall back on this supreme *Ipse dixit*. No amount of difficulty or opposition or apparent failure can abrogate the Church's duty—to preach the Gospel to every

creature. Our Lord has said unto His servants,
" Do this," and they dare not disobey.

It is strange to reflect that the universal
mission of the Church had its birth amid the
most exclusive of ancient nations. In these days
of cosmopolitan sentiment, we fail to realize
how vitally the hope of Israel was bound up with
intense particularism and national pride. No
other lips but Christ's could have uttered His
wonderful edict of comprehension which embraces the Gentile and the barbarian and the
slave as fellow-citizens in the kingdom of God.
We sometimes speak about the solidarity of
mankind as if it were a modern discovery. It
originated in the thought of Jesus Christ. To
Him it appeared a natural fact. He claimed all
human beings for His own by the divine right of
love. Standing there, in poverty and obscurity,
in the corner of a petty Syrian province, He could
look far beyond human prejudices and barriers
and say, quietly and naturally, " The field is the
world."

A plant bears seed spontaneously and multi-
plies unawares. But to make disciples of all
nations has been the deliberate effort and policy
of Christianity. From the very beginning, the
Church realized and responded to its imperial
vocation. Nothing is more impressive in the
Acts of the Apostles than the way in which the
Gospel claims to be universal. Its programme is
one long propaganda. Its message speaks not
to one nation only, but to all kindreds and

peoples ; not in one language, but in the tongues
of the whole world. Christian Missions are a
simple obedience to Christ's explicit and binding
commandment. His followers have gone forth
bearing the precious seed, not because the soil
and the season are attractive, but because He is
Lord of the harvest. " If the Church had
suffered its own love for the world to fix the
limits of its missionary labour, those limits would
have been narrow indeed, and the garner of
God would be empty of sheaves from the wide
field." But at Christ's bidding His people have
gone out into strange lands, not knowing whither
they went, and have embarked on vast enter-
prises, only half conscious of the cost.

Even in its corruptions, Christianity has
never quite lost the universal note. And a real
revival of religion always revives this central
missionary truth, which belongs to the very
genius of the Gospel. As we enter into the
meaning and spirit of our creed, we feel how vital
is this impulse to expansion, how deep in the
heart of faith lies the promise of empire. The
Christian Church lives and moves and has its
being in conquest. When the Gospel ceases to
be a propaganda, it degrades into a superstition
or else it dissolves into a dream. And whenever
the Church repents, and returns to its first love,
it goes back forthwith to recommence its first
work as well—and that work was preaching the
Gospel to every human creature.

Hardly anything about Christ is more wonderful than the way in which He could care at once for the human unit and for the entire human race. His Divine heart could concentrate itself on one poor penitent washing His feet with tears, as though that were the only sin-stricken soul alive. And yet, at the same time, His heart could bear the griefs and carry the sorrows of humanity, until it broke under the burden of the sins of the whole world. Now He clasps a child in His arms, as eagerly as if it were the one solitary lamb which the Good Shepherd came to seek. Now He opens His everlasting arms wide to embrace all souls who like sheep have gone astray. He gazes far beyond the horizon of His disciples into lands undiscovered and nations yet unborn, and He says : " Other sheep I have . . . them also I must bring, . . . and they shall become one flock, one Shepherd."

The Church must share Christ's own spirit— the spirit which cares for each single soul so passionately, and which cares equally for all souls together. As a great preacher has said : " We shall never be able to enter into the depth of Christ's love unless we also enter into its breadth," unless our hearts are enlarged so that we can ratify His saying : " The field is the world." And the true love of souls is no respecter of persons. It disregards the accidents of time and looks at men *sub specie æternitatis,* as they appear in the sight of God. To this love there is neither Greek nor barbarian, neither educated nor ignorant. It can conquer physical repugnance, and forget moral deformity, and lay tender hands on the outcasts and savages and pariahs of mankind. " Can you think," wrote Gordon, from the Sudan, " that God loves those Arabs with the same love as He loves Himself or you ? " Our answer to such a question registers our growth in grace. The Christians who have known most of God have most deeply reverenced human nature, even in its vilest and forlornest specimens. And as we become initiated into the Divine thought and sympathy, we understand why the field can never be any narrower than the world. If Christ has indeed tasted death for every man, surely this awful and glorious fact must be brought home to every man's conscience and heart. The children of His resurrection are trustees, charged to make all nations sharers with us in the immeasurable grace of God.

WE SHALL REAP, IF WE FAINT NOT

No part of the year appears more desolate and depressing than those tardy weeks just before winter has ended, when the earth lies barren and frost-bound and spring is still buried out of sight. And a corresponding season occurs in the spiritual calendar, when after all our patient ploughing and sowing the bleak fields show us no signs of harvest. God's fellow-labourers are tempted to lose heart because the tokens of spiritual success which they long for are withheld

from their eyes. At such a time we may well
confirm and reinforce our faith by the great
apostolic assurance, " In due season we shall
reap, if we faint not." St. Paul's preceding
words, *Be not deceived : God is not mocked* . . .
have been commonly understood as a warning
addressed to evil-doers. But the context shows
that they were written rather as a solemn
encouragement to Christ's disciples, who might
else grow weary of sowing the good seed. This
awful certainty of the spiritual harvest which the
apostle invokes has a twofold aspect. It is like
the pillar of cloud and of fire. And it shines
out as an exceeding great and precious promise
to cheer the dejected and disconsolate people
of God.

To all of us there come seasons in experience
when we feel ready to faint by reason of the sheer
stress and burden of the day. It may be that
our physical energies are flagging, or that our
moral passion has abated, our early enthusiasm
has lost its colour and its zest. The outward
man weakens, and the inward man is not
renewed. Moreover, those Christians who fight
the good fight most manfully become gradually
aware of mighty hostile forces arrayed against
them. They are conscious that the march of
God's kingdom is being strangely arrested and
impeded, if not defeated. The New Testament
never underrates these terrible resources of
Satan. And if there are preachers who ignore
the mysterious evil that is in the world, our

novels and newspapers proclaim it, trumpet-
tongued. The realistic literature of modern
Europe forms a lurid apocalypse of the powers of
darkness which corrupt and enslave mankind.
As we stand face to face with these dreadful
embodiments of iniquity, Christ's bravest soldiers
are sometimes reduced to a kind of dull
despair. How much do our missionary efforts
amount to, after all ? What are we better than
fond, deluded enthusiasts, tempted to whisper,
This also is vanity ?

Those who strive to walk by faith are apt to be
dismayed by the falsehood of appearances. From
the nature of the case their goal and their
recompense lie out of sight. In our earthly
climate the fair fruit of their labour hardly has
time to ripen. And even stout-hearted workers
will faint and grow weary because after long
husbandry they can discern hardly a trace of the
blade and the ear. Nevertheless St. Paul's
confidence remains grounded on the certainty of
the spiritual harvest. Every living seed-germ
carries a miraculous vitality of its own. And so
each drop of the heart's spikenard—concerning
which as it was spilt the cynics cried, " Why
was this waste ? "—becomes a spiritual germ,
fruitful in harvests which shall be garnered
beyond the stars. The evangelist in the market-
place, the colporteur by the roadside, may well
faint and grow weary, but for his assurance that
every word of Divine truth carries its own immortal message, and can spring up and bear

fruit and prosper, he knoweth not how. All seeds germinate best in the dark ; and though now they lie buried away out of sight, yet in due season even we shall reap, if we faint not and scant not our sowing. That which we plant to-day in weakness and dishonour, and water with our tears, God shall raise up in His own power and glory at last.

The same great consoling truth fortifies our courage when we look abroad to contemplate the future of that Church which Christ Himself is building among the nations. Clever, supercilious men of this world go about pronouncing that the Gospel withers and waxes old and is ready to vanish away. Well, one of our own poets reminds us that to contemporaries Christianity has always appeared to be in its decay. To the superior persons who criticize Christian missions, the work of preaching the Gospel to every creature may seem a folly and a failure. They are deceived ; but God is not mocked. The lives of the saints are not foolishness, nor the prayers of the faithful empty breath ; the toil of the missionaries is not wasted, nor the blood of the martyrs shed in vain. For the eternal law of the spiritual harvest holds good concerning what was planted in the Holy Sepulchre. Whatsoever the Lord soweth, that shall He also reap. In that harvest, which is the end of the world, our Redeemer Himself shall be satisfied.

SOME features of the Bible find illustration and commentary in the pages of the *Arabian Nights*. That book, indeed, is the only other example of Oriental literature with which ordinary Englishmen are at all familiar. And though it be far removed from the moral and spiritual standpoint of Holy Scripture, yet it had its origin under the same burning eastern skies, among men of a kindred Semitic race. So we need not wonder that parts of the Bible, like the Book of Esther—not to mention extra-canonical books like Tobit—remind us of the colour and atmosphere and imagery of the *Arabian Nights*. There are sayings in the Gospels of which the same holds good. The parable of the pearl of great price has a real touch of Eastern romance. We picture the roving merchantman who wanders from town to town on his quest; but when at last he lights upon one glorious jewel, he barters away all his lesser gems, he even pawns his baggage and his raiment to buy it, and then tramps home barefooted across the desert with his treasure in his bosom, because he knows that the Caliph will give him a kingdom in exchange.

When our Lord likens the kingdom of heaven to one goodly pearl, many reasons rise up to justify such a comparison. In its origin the pearl differs from every other precious stone. Diamonds and rubies and sapphires are all dead things, literally stones and nothing more. But

pearls are the product of life. Certain kinds of
molluscs secrete these beautiful gems inside
their shells. Apparently some bit of grit or
grain of sand finds its way within the harness of
the oyster, which at once begins to deposit a
nacreous fluid all round the irritating, intrusive
substance, and makes it the nucleus of a pearl.
Perhaps there is a certain fitness in this
comparison of Divine grace, not to the crystal-
line product of blind forces working among dead
atoms, but to the strange result of a living
creature's suffering. Christ likens the purchase
of His Passion to a pearl, which is the costly
burial-place of pain.

Then, among all jewels, the pearl is reckoned
first. Plutarch tells us of the Egyptian queen
who dissolved two magnificent pearls in the glass
with which she pledged her Roman lover. And
from Cleopatra's day until now no other gem
stands before this. Amid changes of fashion
the pearl holds its place, like a monarch whose
courtiers come and go. And the grace of our
Lord Jesus Christ is far above and beyond everything else which life can offer. Art and science
and literature have their own beatitudes, which
men pay a great price to gain : but though they
compete one with another, they are not worthy
to be compared with God's unspeakable gift.

Moreover, the pearl is not only the best
esteemed, but the most beautiful of jewels. The
diamond's flash shows hard and steely, matched
against one drop of morning dew. The ruby

looks dull, compared with a live spark of fire.
The emerald seems tawdry, when you watch
the sunlight streaming through thin wet foliage
after a storm. Even the opal with its iridescent
charm lacks that perfect form, joined with
perfect colour, which makes the pearl pre-
eminent in delicate beauty. Pearl-merchants'
rooms have broad and lofty windows, because
a pearl shows best by daylight and loses under
artificial illumination. So this loveliest jewel
stands aptly for the grace which Christ can
incarnate in human lives. Nothing on earth is
so beautiful as the genuine Christian character.
Sir James Stephen was an avowed agnostic ;
but he confessed that no society of unbelievers
would be able to produce the tone and temper
of noble sanctity which he himself had admired
in a Christian like Frederick Denison Maurice.
Such a character surpasses every other pattern,
because it reflects the likeness of Him Who
descended out of heaven from God. Holiness
needs no artificial radiance : it shows fairest
in the light of common day. But just as even
pearls look most beautiful against a dark background, so the grace of Christ takes added
lustre when it shines out amid sorrow and
gloom. We see then, as never before, the pearl-
like beauty of that spirit which in the sight of
God is of great price.

In earlier ages precious stones were believed
to possess mystic virtues and powers of their
own, just as men ascribed special potencies to the

herbs of the field and the stars of heaven. For example, the amethyst was reputed to be the temperance jewel, which acted as a charm against drunkenness. So a talisman worn in your ring could guard you against poison, or warn you of impending danger, or turn the edge of your foeman's sword. And we may draw a lesson from this ancient superstition that gems have some inherent potency as well as preciousness. The pearl of great price is a true talisman. The Christian who carries it in his heart bears a charmed life. He can be quiet from fear of evil. To him, all things work together for good.

Various names are used to describe the supreme blessing which Christ imparts to the soul. But, like the goodly pearl, this blessing has its price, and its price to each seeker is all that a man hath. And though there may be no outward abandonment of houses or lands or life, the inward surrender of self must be no less real and complete. " Give, and it shall be given unto you " is Christ's inexorable condition. There is no easier way. Yet surely the very cost bears witness to the exceeding and eternal preciousness of what is purchased. There are plenty of mock pearls in the world, cheap enough for anyone who is not ashamed of shams. One test of the true Gospel is the sacrifice which it demands. Nothing exceeds our Lord's infinite rigour, except His infinite mercy. He will not suffer us to keep back any part of the price. There are, indeed, some precious stones which can be subdivided. A great diamond may be cut up into fragments, and each fragment polished into a tiny facsimile of the original gem. But the value of a goodly pearl depends upon its perfect form, and it cannot be sold in fractions. You must take it all in all, or not at all. In this sense we may ask, Is Christ divided ? Can we obey any selection of His commandments, or carry a splinter of His Cross ? God's unspeakable blessing costs exactly as much as we possess, because we must empty ourselves before we can receive it. And if this sound a hard saying, it is the gateway to the happy life.

LIFT UP YOUR HEARTS

A NEW YEAR'S MESSAGE

IN one sense we may speak of every day as the beginning of a year. For man's opportunities, like God's mercies, are new-born with each sunrise. Yet the New Year which changes our dates and our calendars compels us all to think about the silent lapse of that mysterious thing called time. And as we find ourselves standing afresh on the threshold of a shadowy future, we may hear a Voice calling to us from the minarets of heaven with one clear watchword : *Lift up your hearts*.

In some measure at least, all Christians have been redeemed from low-thoughted secularity.

We are not altogether in bondage to the tyranny of " things beneath." We are not quite sunk in selfish indulgence, not quite absorbed in personal ambition, not quite taken up with hunting for social popularity or cheap material success. Yet how many sincere Christians content themselves year after year with a Christian standard which falls miserably below the best. They let themselves be cumbered with worldly cares and hampered with worldly gear. They settle down into dull spiritual mediocrity. They are deaf to the upward calling of God in Christ Jesus.

To bring about such a state of soul many causes combine. Do not multitudes of well-meaning, orthodox people become enslaved by their own religious routine ? Custom—even Church custom—lies upon them like a weight. Mere use and wont have dulled their inward sense until they hardly even aspire to rise above the level of the commonplace. They have lost power to lift up their hearts from the conventional to the ideal. They have no real faith in the unexplored possibilities of Christian experience. They hardly ever hunger and thirst after the glorious liberty of the children of God. So many persons, especially in middle life, though they are sincere in the Christian confession, become fatalistic in regard to the Christian character. They sink into a kind of spiritual inertia, and persuade themselves that they are the victims of circumstances and of temperament. Others, again, try to live on the

recollection of their earlier religious history.
They rely upon some inward grace which God
granted them many years ago. They sit mum-
bling the remainder-biscuit of this bygone
experience, instead of gathering the daily manna
which falls fresh as morning dew from heaven.

To all such as these—the conventionalist, the
torpid, the self-satisfied—the Divine challenge
is sounding : " Life up your hearts." As the
New Year dawns, God is calling each of us to rise
into new expectancy, new consecration, new
ventures of faith. His Will has grander, richer
experiences waiting for us in days to come—a
purer vision, a statelier rapture, a holier
sacrifice, a deeper beatitude. That point of
attainment in the past which seemed our limit
and boundary shall prove only the peak in some
spiritual Darien, from which we gaze out upon
a new ocean of peace and joy as yet unpossessed.
There must be no finality in our Christian ambition, for there are no limits to the blessing
which rewards an eager and obedient heart.
Great expectations would make us all saints : for
in the kingdom of heaven great expectations are
never disappointed.

And even devoted Christian workers may learn
to lift up their hearts in fresh service for the cause
and the Church of God. There come moments
when the most successful soldiers are tempted to
rest on their laurels, and the most strenuous
labourers feel that they have reached the end of
their strength, and the most generous givers are

apt to feel as though they have no more spikenard left. Then is the time for us to lift up our
hearts to Him Who replenishes His servants'
store with grace added to grace, Who reveals
wiser and worthier methods and imparts more
abundant fortitude. Whether Christ send us
out into the wilderness after His lost sheep, or
trust us with His lambs to carry in our arms
at home, let us lift up our hearts to Him in
passionate desire that we may share in the
eternal cure of souls wherein the Lord Himself
fainteth not neither is weary, so long as souls are
left shepherdless and forlorn. In proportion as
we obey the call of the Crucified Who beckons
us to His side, saying, " Come up hither," we
learn from Him the Divine secrets of devotion,
until we too become brave for love's sake to give
ourselves away.

Above all the conflict and dimness of this lower
world where we sit despondent and downhearted,
we know that Christ Himself is reigning and
conquering, and bringing time's mysterious
travail to an appointed end. In spite of our
defeats, our disappointments, our failures, He
must reign till He hath put all enemies under
His feet. Therefore, as we hear the watchword, *Lift up your hearts*, we take courage to
answer with the Church's ancient antiphon:
" We lift them up unto the Lord."

WITH FEAR AND TREMBLING

IN one of Emerson's essays he utters a clarion
call to self-reliance : " Trust thyself," he cries ;
" every heart vibrates to that iron string."
But Emerson's message is only a fragment of the
Gospel. Human nature has no power to deliver
and redeem itself. And so while the New
Testament says, " Work out your own salvation
with fear and trembling," it makes haste to add,
" for it is God which worketh in you both to will
and to do of His good pleasure." The history
of humanity is one long confession that, left
alone, men only avail to work out their own
failure ; while all the saints tell us that they
have overcome the world only in so far as they
were inspired and sustained and consoled by the
succours of Divine grace. Their victory is not
theirs, but the work in them of Another.

Salvation, to a Christian, is much more than
self-culture. It is not merely the development
of original and native virtues. It means the
actual infusion and impartation of goodness from
a Source beyond ourselves. The Christian life
is begun, continued, and completed in supernatural grace. Nothing else makes it possible.
The simplest Christian knows that to live according to the Sermon on the Mount for a single day
far exceeds his natural human energies. But
the power of an endless Life is poured into each
faithful heart, and transfigures the whole
moral nature, and works out salvation in it and

for it which it could never effect alone. Here
is the sole ground of our Christian hope and
confidence. Nothing except grace accounts for
the patience and perseverance of the saints.
But they take courage to labour on, seeing that
God Himself is working in the secret springs of
their will.

The watershed which divides believers from
unbelievers is this doctrine of supernatural
grace. Calvinists and Romanists have disputed
for centuries as to the channels and conditions
whereby God's grace is conveyed to man. But
they are absolutely at one as to the reality of
this gift on God's part and as to the need of
it on man's part. They all hope to work out
their own salvation only by the efficacy of the
Holy Ghost. To believe in grace, to experience
its reality, to grasp its unseen strength—here
is the touchstone of Christian life in the soul.

" Work out your own salvation *with fear and
trembling*." Those last four words are not,
perhaps, what we might expect. The Apostle
does not say, " Work, therefore, boldly, joyfully,
exultantly " ; he says, " with fear and trembling." One reason for the warning may be
that he has so sublime an estimate of what salvation involves, and at the same time so profound
a sense of what perdition would entail. And in
truth, when we consider the seriousness of life
and its issues, the nameless perils of moral shipwreck, we may well pause in fear and trembling
lest, after all, any of us should be a castaway.

A further ground for this trembling appears when we feel how awful it is to become a partner and fellow-worker with God Himself. This alliance of our spirits with the Almighty and All-holy Spirit is the closest and most intimate companionship. There was a German mystic who declared that he could feel the whole six days' work of creation going on in his own breast. The Christian realizes, not without fear and trembling, that he is inhabited and controlled by the very presence of the living God.

And yet perhaps the Apostle, when he bids us tremble and fear, is thinking rather of the wonder and glory of salvation itself, the amazing destiny which opens out before each redeemed soul. That heavenly prize matters so unspeakably that a man may well tremble as he thinks about it. To believe that some day even we shall be made pure in heart, that we shall enter on the beatific vision of God, that we shall love as we are loved, and know as we are known —it makes us afraid. Sydney Dobell speaks somewhere about the Indian traveller who trembles as he buys a kingdom for a bead. And when we begin to understand how much salvation means, and how little we ever do, or can do, to win it, we grow simply breathless with awe.

Most Christians will admit that the spiritual experiences described in the New Testament are pitched in a transcendent key. Sometimes, however, we lose sight of the fact that our Christian service is pitched in the very same key, and that we dare not lower it or tone it down. The Church's labour, as well as the Church's communion, must walk by the same supernatural rule—*Dei gratiâ*. There is no other way. Our missionary enterprise can persist and prosper and triumph solely by Divine grace. The growth of the kingdom of God can never be gauged by the standards of worldly common sense. Concerning the progress of the Church universal—just as much as concerning the salvation of any sinful soul—we have to say humbly and reverently, " By grace . . . and that not of yourselves ; it is the gift of God."

THE CROSS MADE PLAIN IN THE HEART

WHEN we study the Evangelists, we discover that they occupy between a quarter and a third of their whole space with the narrative of Passion week and its sequel. They felt that the rest of our Lord's life formed a prelude and preparation for that last act in which He laid it down. Yet the space which the Crucifixion fills in our own Christian thought and feeling will vary at different stages in the experience of life. Good Friday means little to those who are young. They are still in their first garden, and it perplexes them to find the Cross set up among the flowers. That Cross speaks in a dark language which they have not mastered, a language whose grammar they have not had time to learn. " A simple child, that lightly draws its breath, and feels its life in every limb, what should it know of death ? " What should it know of the sting of death, which is sin ? What should it know of the Conqueror of death, Who put away sin by the sacrifice of Himself ?

Then, as the years pass, we grow older and less innocent and more aware of the evil and misery in the world. And we discover a strange new significance in the Figure of the Man of Sorrows. Every trial we encounter, every tear we shed, every pang we suffer, every loss we undergo, becomes a fresh lesson in the sacred meaning of Good Friday. To shallow, uninstructed souls, that day falls like a blot on the fair spring sunshine. But in God's education of His children there are multitudes who learn to measure the heights and depths of existence, after they have been initiated into the secrets of suffering. And these can enter into part of the meaning of the Passion of Jesus Christ.

When we find ourselves disappointed by people whom we had trusted and betrayed by our own familiar friends, we begin to realize a little of what was done in the moonlight under the olives of Gethsemane. When we stand deserted and forsaken in our dreariest and loneliest hour, we begin to feel what it must have meant when they all forsook Him and fled. Even the details of the Divine Passion assume deeper meaning as we learn to interpret them by our own experiences, after we have trodden for ourselves some steps along the *Via Dolorosa*. When we have been despised and rejected of men, when they have gambled away our credit and parted the seamless robe of our reputation, when the sun hides its face from our anguish, then the Divine words spoken from the Cross come home to us with new and piercing truth.

For instance, as years go by, we discover how many wrongs we are called upon to endure and to forgive. We recognize, too, how often those who injure us are blind to their own injustice, how those who wound us most sorely are but half-conscious of their own cruelty. Then we begin in some dim fashion to guess the greatness of that prayer : " Forgive them, for they know not what they do." And when for the first time we have seen a man die—of all events the most hackneyed, and most solemn— when we have stood breathless to watch him sob out his parting breath, then we find how much is contained in the sentences concerning the Son of God—" It is finished," and " He gave up the ghost." It is a familiar experience that the older we grow the more funerals we have to follow. But only after we have been bidden to many burials and have made pilgrimage to many sepulchres, do we realize how much it means that Christ Himself was buried, and that His holy sepulchre is an empty grave.

Deep calleth unto deep, throughout this awful Passion Music, and deep answereth unto deep. The anguish and agony of the Cross correspond with the profoundest experiences of our mortality. When we " turn from life's most perplexed and sorrowful contradictions to the eyes and brow of Him who was indeed acquainted with grief, we meet there with a look of solemn recognition," we hear from the lips of the Crucified the only words which speak to the heart of the world : *Comfort ye, comfort ye my people, saith your God*. His Cross is the justification of a suffering world. Surely He hath borne our griefs, and carried our sorrows. He has taken all those things in themselves most terrible, which seem to contradict and deny God's goodness, and He has made those very things the proofs and tokens of Almighty Love, poured out with infinite joy for us and for our salvation.

Yet to say thus much, only touches the fringe of the total truth. The same gradual experience and discipline of life which initiate us into the secret of sorrow, unfold to us as well the mystery of sacrifice and expiation. Here again the young, the innocent, the happy must needs stand aloof and apart. They have hardly tasted the tree of the knowledge of good and evil ; they have not learned yet what it means to be convinced of sin, and of righteousness, and of judgment to come. But as the inward Teacher brings home to our consciences the

dreadful realities of guilt and remorse and condemnation, we gain some glimmering of the
eternal spiritual order. Behind these earthly
shadows we catch a vision of the great White
Throne. And then we realize that nothing else
matters for us, except that we sinners should be
set right with our God. Hence it is that the
truest Christians have always been preoccupied
with the mystery of the Divine Sacrifice for the
reversal and retrieval of human guilt. The dying
of the Son of God stands for that Passion of
everlasting Love which has dealt with our evil
and undone our ill-doing—yea, has borne away
the sin of the whole world.

From its very nature, the Crucifixion can only
be apprehended in terms of our own deepest
experiences. When the final earthly change falls
upon each man, when he passes through the
valley of the shadow of death—then, and not till
then, does he understand how much the death
of Jesus Christ means. But in the act and
article of dying, Good Friday will seem to us the
day of days, worth all other days put together.
When the holiest Christians draw near their
exodus, it is very wonderful how their thoughts
and hopes turn by instinct, not to the heaven
which they are approaching, but to the victorious Death which opened the kingdom of
heaven to all believers. " Hold Thou Thy Cross
before my closing eyes "—that is the saint's
last prayer. The supreme effort of a faithful
soul is to lift itself up towards Him Who was

lifted up. In the hour of death and in the day of judgment, *Rock of Ages, let me hide myself in Thee*.

WE STOOP TO RISE

IN the Church's calendar, one day has been set apart which is still observed by multitudes of Christian people all the world over as the festival of our Lord's ascension into heaven. Ascension Day not only reminds us of an article in our creed ; it suggests the eternal scope and value of the Lord's saying in the Gospel, *He that humbleth himself shall be exalted*. For Christ Himself becomes the cardinal example of His own words. So it is written, " He humbled Himself . . . wherefore also God hath highly exalted Him." " Now this, He ascended, what is it but that He also descended into the lower parts of the earth ? " When the Eternal Son was made flesh and entered the world of time He went down into the nethermost depths of human evil and misery. He Who was in the form of God, yet counted it not a prize to be on an equality with God, but emptied Himself, taking the form of a slave, and being found in fashion as a man, He humbled Himself, becoming obedient unto death, yea, the death of the Cross. Redemption began with the immeasurable self-abasement of the Redeemer. The All-Holy has taken upon Himself our shame and guilt. The All-Blessed has agonized under our evil. The King of kings has

7

made Himself a servant of servants. The
Immortal Love has tasted death for us all. He
chose to stoop. He endured a self-beggary so
absolute, a descent so profound, that when we
try to fathom its meaning, we can only whisper
in amazement and adoration, " O the depth ! "

There is nothing else like this descent, nothing
which we can match against it and compare with
it, in history or legend or poet's dream. In
human experience, indeed, we find examples of
men coming down from the high places to the
low places of the world. For the most part they
do it reluctantly, out of compulsion—through
some sudden accident, or calamity, or ruin. A
man, for instance, who has moved in exalted
circles forfeits caste and character ; he sinks
down to hide in obscurity, and begins with shame
to take the lowest seat. Sometimes we witness
tragic humiliations such as these : the famous
singer starves in a garret, the bankrupt million-
aire takes refuge in a workhouse, the faithless
prophet dies in a gaol.

Yet again, there may be condescension which
is voluntary and deliberate—as when a clever
man adapts himself to dull wits ; or a teacher
simplifies his thoughts and words for his simplest
pupils ; or a father and mother humble their
minds to match the mind of their little child.

And we may find nobler instances still among
the disciples of Him Who descended. The
imitation of Christ has not died out. There are
Christians who have joyfully followed their

Master in this, and have gone down after Him into the depths of poverty and misery for the sake of the bodies and spirits which are imprisoned there. High-bred men and women have left empty the chief seats in the synagogues, and deserted the uppermost rooms at the feasts, and resigned the best society and the finest culture. They have done this so that they might live among the ignorant, and make friends with the lonely, and comfort the sorrowful, and become of no reputation for the sake of the disreputable, and be kind to the unthankful and the evil.

In recent years, indeed, a species of self-humiliation has to some extent become a fashion, almost a fad. People who consider themselves to belong to the upper classes have gone down to mix with what they call the lower orders, and even lodged awhile in mean back-streets. They do it from mingled motives—some out of genuine pity and interest, others to make an experiment in social theories, others to find a stimulus to jaded sensations, others to rake up copy for a novel out of the lower parts of the earth. And though they may fail to effect much good, they can hardly escape learning some wholesome lessons.

But the capital defect about most abnegations of this kind is just here : they somehow seem forced, and constrained, and unnatural. Such persons constantly feel, and make their neighbours feel also, that they *have* descended. It is a

condescension on their part ; and this taints their
sacrifice.　They stoop ; but they are consciously
superior persons all the time.　No spirit can be
more utterly alien to the heart of God.　Surely
Jesus Christ nailed the sin of condescension to
His own Cross.　The supreme quality about our
Lord's humiliation was its perfect naturalness.
He stooped without an effort.　He forgot to
count how much it cost.　People never felt
that He was dragging Himself down to their
level.　He took the lowest place because He
was indeed lowly in heart.　When Christ descended to the nethermost parts of the earth,
men recognized that He was really at home there
—nay, they cast it at Him that He went to His
own place.　The Pharisees pointed the finger of
scorn, and whispered that He chose the company
He was fit for—this Friend of publicans and
sinners !

　Surely our Lord is most Divine in this, that
His great humility belongs to His very nature.
He descended, by the natural instinct of love ;
and so also, He ascended.　The humiliation and
the resurrection were alike normal in regard to
Himself, and congruous with His own character.
In the New Testament, Easter and Ascension
Day occur as a natural climax.　They are
represented to us not as sudden portents, but
rather as a Divine necessity.　Thus it behoved
Him to suffer, and to rise from the dead.　His
rising was as inevitable as His stooping.　He
rose " as a man rises in the morning when he

awakes and sleep passes from him." He rose from the bondage of corruption, because *it was not possible for Him to be holden thereby.*

The resurrection and ascension of our Lord are in correspondence with the spiritual law—*He that humbleth himself shall be exalted.* In the kingdom of heaven, it perpetually comes true that the way upward lies first downward, that the valley of humiliation is the only road by which we travel to the sky. Whereas those who sink themselves and forget themselves for the sake of Christ's little ones are astonished to find greatness thrust upon them in the will and counsel of God. The history of the Church and the testimony of the saints ratify the same spiritual lesson. When George Herbert sings in his Easter hymn :

> " Rise heart ; thy Lord is risen,"

we may venture to add another line—

> " Stoop heart ; thy Lord hath stooped."

THE EARNEST OF OUR INHERITANCE

In his Epistle to the Ephesians, St. Paul speaks of the Holy Spirit of promise which is an earnest of our inheritance ; and he repeats almost the same words when he tells the Corinthians that God hath " given us the earnest of the Spirit in our hearts "—that is, the earnest which consists

of the Spirit. The old Saxon word is simple
enough. An earnest means a pledge—something which a man gives you to prove that he is
in earnest ; like the deposit or caution money
put down by a purchaser at a sale, or the
guarantee required from a contractor who undertakes some public work.

We may find still homelier illustrations of an
earnest. In my native county, when a mistress
hired a servant, after they had agreed about the
wages to be given and the service required, it
was the custom for the mistress to give the maid
a shilling or a half-crown, and that coin was
called an earnest : it sealed the bargain. In
former days, when a man sold a meadow, held
under a certain kind of land-tenure, the seller
would cut a grass sod out of that field and
lifting the sod with his own hands would deliver
it over into the purchaser's. That grass sod was
the earnest of the inheritance—a sample and a
pledge of the land sold ; and the transfer of the
sod from seller to buyer sealed the bargain and
made it valid in law. Examples like these
explain the Apostle's words and point towards
his meaning.

In England the weeks before Easter are full
of earnests. What is spring-time but the
earnest of an inheritance of flowers and foliage
not seen as yet ? Under all the hedgerows in
April, on every bank and bush, the young shoots
are writing their green promise, " It doth not
yet appear what we shall be." You find a

throstle's nest ; those blue eggs are the earnest of how much music. You stand under a spreading chestnut tree ; those thick brown buds are the earnest of what a royal wealth of blossom, when after many days the tree sends up incense from all its spires. One swallow does not make a summer—but when we see the first swallow we know that summer is nigh, even at the door. Spring herself seems to whisper : " If I go not away summer will not come. Behold I bring you some better thing, without which your inheritance cannot be made perfect."

These things are an allegory. We are saved by hope. Sometimes it is hope deferred ; yet we never doubt that nature's earnests will come true at last. She will certainly do for us all those things of which she has spoken to us in the spring. And our God, Who is the Maker and Master of all worlds—shall He be less faithful to carry out the forecasts of His mercy, to fulfil the promises of His love ? He Who has begun a good work in us, shall doubtless make it perfect against the day of Christ. Already He has given us His Spirit, for the earnest of our inheritance. We carry in our hearts the pledge and the token, the sample and the security, of those heavenly things which He hath prepared for them that love Him and wait for Him according to His word.

We see thus that an earnest involves two ideas : it is a sample and a security. It is not only the pattern, it is the pledge of what is yet

to be.   The Divine Spirit already within is our
security for a Divine future waiting beyond.
Christ's argument for immortality against the
Sadducees hinges upon this point.   The God of
Abraham, and of Isaac, and of Jacob !   Now
God is not the God of dead men, but of living
men.   A soul which can enter into God's friendship is henceforth no mere slave of time and
sense.   Such a Divine relation implies an eternal
bond.   The Spirit prophesies the inheritance.

We may put it in another way, and affirm
that with God to begin always means to finish.
The first operations of His grace carry the promise and potency of their own completion.   The
Author of our faith must needs be its Perfecter
as well.   When we sing the old hymn " O
Lord, my best desires fulfil "—do we stop to ask
where those desires came from, and what they
portend ?   Why did God breathe them into our
souls ?   Was it only to tantalize us with their
vanity ?   Was it not to fulfil them abundantly
at last, when we have been made patient and
they have been made pure.   The poet who
tells how " our life is plagued with dreams of
something sweet," only echoes the sentence of
the Apostle " The earnest expectation of the
creature waits for the manifestation of the sons
of God."

The real test of any life is its expectancy.
People write epitaphs on the men who have
achieved great things on earth, and say they are
gone to their reward.   But man's spirit, not his

achievement, is the earnest of his inheritance—not what he actually grasped, but what he planned and willed and yearned after and longed for and strove to reach, and was never granted in this life to attain. Men's failures are often far more prophetic, far more consoling, than what we reckon as their successes. Spirits are not finely touched but to fine issues—albeit those issues lie in heavenly places out of sight. " What I aspired to be, and was not, comforts me." For it is an earnest of my inheritance in the spiritual city, where, as Dante said, to will and to do are the same.

WHEN GOD SPEAKS TWICE

THE Bible throughout builds upon one great assumption. It takes for granted that God does actually speak to men. The Gospel postulates the reality of Divine communications. It is not we who grope after God, and find Him by our searching : it is God Who discovers Himself to us, and finds us, and lays hold on us. There is an awful simplicity and directness about a Divine message. God calleth His own by name. His Voice singles a man out from the crowd, and isolates him from all other souls in the world. It makes a desert round him in the midst of the market-place and brings him alone, face to face, with his Maker. And again, God's appeal is not only real and simple and personal ; it is also reiterated. The Lord's entreating is like His forgiving—until seventy times seven. When we pray to Him, He bids us use no vain repetitions. But in His words to us it seems sometimes as though God did seek to be heard for His much speaking. *God speaketh once, yea twice— though man regardeth it not.*

Now when you call anyone by name, and repeat the name, it is because you are deeply in earnest, because what you have to say is urgent. Men speak once, yea twice, when they speak in the language of passion or in the accents of grief and despair. So King Lear cried to the daughter whom he held dead in his arms :

"*Cordelia, Cordelia, stay a little.*"

And so that other royal father lamented in the like bitterness of bereavement : " O my son Absalom ! my son, my son Absalom ! would God I had died for thee, O Absalom, my son, my son ! "

We may turn to some examples in Scripture of how God Himself spoke to men, and spoke repeatedly : how He called them not once but twice, reiterating their name. So it was with Moses, when he drew near to the bush that burned with fire, and God called unto him out of the midst of the bush : " Moses, Moses," and he said : " Here am I." The Divine Word came with such solemn emphasis, because it had to reveal the Divine Presence in a place and in a form where God was least expected. Even so He still

tries to arouse our attention, as He repeats our
name amid humble surroundings and in commonplace duties, making us aware that the very
place where we stand—the shop where we work,
the home where we dwell, the chamber where
we kneel—is holy ground.

So it was with Samuel, when he lay down to
sleep, and the Lord came and called : "Samuel,
Samuel." The Voice sounded peremptory—as
one might summon a servant to receive an
order ; but the message came, not when the
sacrifice was smoking on the altar and the silver
trumpets blew for a solemn feast, but when the
child who ministered to Eli lay quietly slumber-
ing. Even so the Holy Spirit often draws near
to us in our quietness, and the word of His will is
uttered in the heart of that servant who is
humble to listen and swift to obey.

So it was with Abraham, at the trial of his
faith on the hill of Moriah, when the angel of the
Lord called and said : "Abraham, Abraham "—
an urgent summons, to check him at the last
moment from the sacrifice he was offering. And
still there are times when God's voice comes
to us to rectify our religious judgments. For
He is not only the Author of our conscience ;
He is its Perfecter as well. When we are following some line of custom or tradition which seems
consecrated as our duty, His warning whisper
shows us a purer goodness, or a truer truth, or a
more acceptable service. We learn, as the
patriarch learned, that the sacrifices of God are a

broken spirit ; and we bind upon His altar our own pride and self-will.

So it was with Simon Peter when Christ warned him on the very night of the denial : " Simon, Simon, behold Satan hath desired to have you, that he may sift you as wheat." We can hear the iteration of anxiety, bidding the apostle who standeth to take heed lest he fall. For the virtue on which we pride ourselves is always the very point on which we are most apt to give way ; and the temptation which masters us is the temptation against which we feel most secure.

So it was with the sister of Lazarus at Bethany, in the house where Christ was most at home. To her he said : " Martha, Martha, thou art careful and troubled about many things." That repetition was half in tenderness, half in rebuke. But the rebuke might well be addressed to many a modern Christian who is distracted and dissipated by his own good works. In the stress of our religious and philanthropic activities, we may still find that " doing is a deadly thing." We still need to be recalled to the one thing needful, to the good part of communion with Christ—which is so good, because it shall never be taken away.

And so it was with the young Pharisee riding to Damascus, when he saw a light above the brightness of the sun, and heard a Voice say, " Saul, Saul, why persecutest thou Me ? " We have three different accounts of that memorable vision, and each one of them preserves the detail of the doubly-repeated name. Our Lord's reproach was blended with compassion, and His remonstrance was not so much sternness as pity : " Thou art persecuting Me ; but it is hard for thee. Thou art wounding thyself against the pricks."

Finally, we note that this Voice from heaven, which smote down Saul the Pharisee to the earth, was not any strange inarticulate thunder ; it came, as he says himself, speaking to him " in the Hebrew tongue "—in the mother-tongue in which he had been cradled. So easy, so familiar is the language of the Highest with His children. God becomes all things to all men, if by any means He may win some. And we repeat His Gospel as He would have it repeated, when we help every man to receive that Divine Word in the speech wherein he was born.

THE HILLS AND THE VALLEYS

AHAB, king of Israel, had been shut up and besieged in Samaria by Benhadad, king of Syria. The city was on the brink of surrender when a sudden desperate sally by the remnant of Israel routed the huge Syrian host and drove them back to their own land. Benhadad's captains thereupon tried to explain away the disaster. Beaten captains always do. A war office was

never yet bankrupt of excuses. These Syrians
fell back on the primitive pagan doctrine of a
tribal deity, whose rights and powers ended
outside the borders of his chosen people. As the
land of Israel was full of crags and mountains,
the god of Israel seemed naturally a god of the
hills ; while the Syrians, who dwelt in a country
of rich river-plains, might believe that their god
was a god of the valleys, whose power they left
behind them when they invaded the highlands
of Palestine. Benhadad's captains caught at
this theory in order to cover their own defeat.
They said : " The god of Israel is a god of the
hills ; therefore they were stronger than we ;
but let us fight against them in the plain, and
surely we shall be stronger than they."

In our ears the Syrian superstition sounds half-
childish ; and yet many a modern Christian
practically worships a local and limited deity
in the primitive pagan way. Observe, for
example, how some people behave when they go
away from home. Holiday-makers too often
carry out that proverb which was coined by the
medieval pilgrims : " You must do at Rome
as the Romans do." There are many tourists
who seem to change their characters when once
they get outside their own country. Dr. Jekyll
in England becomes Mr. Hyde when he goes
abroad. What sad self-betrayals we sometimes
witness on an ocean steamer or at a foreign
hotel !

There are many other obvious illustrations of

the same unspiritual heresy. How often we are tempted to treat God as the God of Sundays, but not the God of week-days ; the God of the church, but not the God of the market-place and the counting-house and the railway train ; the God of the ancient prophet, but not the God of the modern politician ; the God of the Bible, but not the God of novels and newspapers.

Sometimes, again, this Syrian heresy takes a Manichean disguise—as though the God of the soul were not the God of the body. But the God of our work is also the God of our play. The God of the oratory is also the God of the gymnasium and the cricket-field. *Forasmuch as the children are partakers of flesh and blood, He also Himself likewise took part of the same*. The mystery of the Incarnation has shown us, once and for ever, that we should call nothing common or unclean—nothing, except sin.

The same Syrian heresy, the belief in a partial God, warps our judgment in regard to the high-lands and the lowlands of human life. Here is a man of lofty genius, a poet, an artist, who stands exalted above the crowd. We suppose, there-fore, that he is above the common law which binds the crowd ; he may neglect the ordinary humdrum moralities ; he is too eminent to be judged by the Ten Commandments. Then, again, there is the opposite extreme, also fashion-able to-day—the notion that you can hardly expect a man to be a Christian unless he has a certain amount of comfort and leisure and education. There are modern philanthropists who will excuse almost any baseness in anybody, if he be only poor enough. But in the common salvation there is no difference. The God of high life is also the God of low life. The gulf between right and wrong is no deeper in the West End than it is in the East End. Christ comes to our back door as often as He comes to our front door. The Real Presence is no more in the parlour than in the kitchen—no more, but no less. Duty is just as eternally and inexorably binding on a poor man as on a rich man. Selfishness is a deadly sin, whether you find it in a prince or a peasant. Class jealousy is a vile passion, whether it exists in a trades' union or in a house of peers. There is no respect of persons with God.

This truth applies to the ups and downs of our personal experience. The God of prosperity is also the God of adversity. He is in our health ; He is in our sickness too. He is in our successes ; He is not less surely in what we call our failures. Behold, all things come from Him ; He grants, and He refuses ; He gives, and He takes away ; He casteth down, and He lifteth up ; and our time and strength and wisdom, our plans and patience—how vain they all are, except as the instruments of His holy and acceptable and perfect Will.

The same truth holds good not only regarding outward circumstances, but in the realm of inward experience. A buoyant soul is indeed a great blessing. But to few of us is it granted " to live on the crest of the wave " : far oftener we find ourselves floating in the hollow of its trough. Yet the God of exultation is also the God of depression. He is in the high ecstasy of that spiritual crisis, in the noble glow of that great decision. He is not less surely in our lowliest duties, in our daily drudgeries, in the dull, drab, commonplace monotony of our lives.

The Author of faith is Himself also its Sustainer, and its Finisher. Each pilgrim's progress is begun, continued, and ended in Him ; and no one step of the way is more divine than any other. The God of the delectable mountains, from whose shining summits we see the land that is very far off, is also the God of the valley of humiliation ; and a faithful pilgrim who goes down into its shadows can whisper, " The day is Thine, the night also is Thine : the darkness and the light are both alike to Thee." Surely it comforts us to know that the God of the wicket-gate is also the God of the dark river. The same Lord, in Whom we live and move and have our being now, is He in whose arms we shall lie back to die at last. *Living, therefore, or dying, we are the Lord's.*

IF THOU KNEWEST

HARDLY any episode in the Gospels is more familiar than the dialogue by the well-side

8

between Christ and the woman of Samaria.
The Evangelist brings out a dramatic feature in
the situation—the irony of her unconscious
ignorance. We are in the secret : we understand
who is this Stranger, begging that He may quench
His thirst. But the woman sees only a casual
Jewish pilgrim, and begrudges Him a cup of
cold water. Her attitude is a parable, to teach
us how blindly we too may miss our benedictions. The Traveller unknown meets us on life's
journey, the mysterious Companion walks along
the path by our side : but our eyes are holden.
Alas ! that so often we must lament too late,
when the day of our visitation is ended, " Surely
the Lord was in this place ; and I knew it not."

The same dimness of spiritual vision which
makes us unaware of things eternal besets us
behind and before and hinders us on every side.
We may be too dull to discern the good gift
of God even when it enters under our roof and
takes its place by our own fireside. To enter-
tain unrecognized angels is so fatally easy, and
so miserably common. Consider only one instance. The book of all others which you are
most likely to find somewhere in an Englishman's
home is the New Testament. But how many
Englishmen realize what the New Testament
contains and what it discloses ? Even when it
is read, the veil is upon their heart. Would they
leave it unstudied and unpondered if they had
an inkling of the sacred treasure which its pages
enshrine ? This Book which is above every book

cries out against its unworthy possessor, and
says : *If thou knewest the gift of God.*

The experience of the Samaritan woman by
Jacob's well is a picture to show us how God's
grace comes concealed in every call to un-
selfish service. In one sense the service of
others may be described as a sacrament—because it can reveal the Real Presence. The Lord
Himself drew near to that sinful alien woman,
appealing for personal help : " Give Me to drink."
And His request carried in itself an unspeakable
blessing. She was isolated by the triple prejudices of sex and race and creed. The Divine
Mercy approached her in a simple human plea
for human kindness. Even so our wayside
duties and charities can become channels of
heavenly ministry to our own souls. The
appeal for pity, the demand for self-denial, which
come knocking at the door of the conscience—
how strangely different they would sound if we
knew Who it is that saith to us, speaking by the
lips of His disconsolate and disinherited, " Give
Me to drink." When some fresh claim for
service lays its hand upon us, we are tempted to
murmur, " O hard requirement ! " But the angels
are singing, " O blessed opportunity ! " The
very grace which your spirit pines after and
vainly searches hither and thither to find—that
grace meets you face to face, disguised as the
least of Christ's little ones who pleads for a cup
of cold water. In such a request and its fulfilment, you may realize the gift of God. In such

a demand and its refusal you may forfeit life's supreme opportunity—and wake up at last among those condemned who ask in their bewilderment, " Lord, when saw we Thee athirst ? "

Yet we err when we speak of the Gospel as though it imposes a claim, and not as if it bestows a gift. We do not know Christ so long as we think of Him as an austere man, taking up where He laid not down, and gathering where He has not strawed—One Who makes hard and exacting demands upon His disciples, instead of One Who pours Himself out with infinite bounty and satisfies every deepest need and secret desire of the soul. The Incarnation and Advent proclaim how *God so loved that He gave.* Now the spiritual value of any offering which we can make one to another consists in this : how far does the present express and convey the very heart of the donor, how far is it a part of himself which he bestows ? And here is the infinite, unexpressible quality of the gift of God : He gave His only begotten Son, Who is part of Himself. Men have sometimes doubted whether they dare confess Christ to be of one nature and one substance with the Father. But surely that doctrine which makes Him no more than a demi-god dims and tarnishes the glory of the Divine self-sacrifice. No lower Person could suffice for man's redemption. No meaner Gift could reveal the secret of the Eternal Heart.

Let us cease therefore to murmur or to

marvel because God's revelation is too profound for our analysis, because it transcends our definitions. St. Paul could not argue about the Gospel with hard logic, as some cold-blooded theologians have tried to reason. At the climax of his grandest arguments the apostle breaks off, and adds in a whisper, " O the depth ! " " Behold I show you a mystery ! " " The Love which passeth knowledge." Even so, as we join the anthem, " Blessed be the Lord God of Israel, for He hath visited and redeemed His people," we go on humbly to confess with awe and amazement and adoration : *Thanks be unto God for His unspeakable Gift.*

OUR HOPE FOR YEARS TO COME

In the New Testament the word hope occurs in two senses. Sometimes it stands for the object of our expectancy—the hope laid up for us in heaven. More often, however, it means the attitude or bearing on our part, which corresponds to that object and is governed by it—the temper which answers to and embraces great and worthy things hoped for. In this sense the apostle reckons hope among the cardinal Christian virtues. And the masters of spiritual experience teach us that no grace is more vital for Christian progress and victory. They agree that we are saved by hope. Herein, they say, is our cure for disappointment, our secret of endurance, our antidote against dismay.

Nevertheless the Bible, and the profoundest students of the Bible, will not encourage us in cheap and easy optimism. Consider, for example, the teaching of the *Pilgrim's Progress*. It may have been partly John Bunyan's personal temperament which drew him towards types of character like Mr. Despondency and his daughter Much-afraid. And in the second part of the *Pilgrim's Progress* the principal figure is Mr. Fearing, " one of the most troublesome pilgrims that ever I met with in all my days." At the Slough of Despond he lay for above a month, till " one sunshiny morning, I scarce know how, he ventured and got over. But when he was over, he could scarce believe it. He had, I think, a Slough of Despond in his mind, a Slough that he carried everywhere with him." As he stood shaking and shrinking at the Wicket Gate, " it would have pitied one's heart to have seen him." He was dejected at every difficulty, and stumbled at every straw that anybody cast in his way. In the Valley of the Shadow he was ready to die for fear. Once within the Interpreter's House he fared better ; for the Interpreter " being very tender, specially to them that are afraid . . . carried it wonderful lovingly to him." But at the River, Mr. Fearing was in a heavy case ; now, now, he said he should be drowned for ever, and so never see that Face with comfort that he had come so

many miles to behold. Yet it was remarkable
that the water of the River was lower at that
time than it had been in the memory of man,
and so he went over at last not much above
wet-shod.

Now there are multitudes of modern pilgrims
who belong to the spiritual family of Mr. Fearing.
They would shrink from confessing themselves
to be daunted and dismayed : but they are
secretly conscious that this is their condition—
most of all when they pause for a moment on
the threshold of a shadowy future and gaze
wistfully into the unknown years before them.
We live in times which may excuse foreboding
and misgiving. Amid wars and rumours of wars
and tumults of nations, it is not strange to find
men's hearts failing them for fear. And in
our own spiritual experience—when we recall
our sloth and coldness and meanness, our waver-
ing purposes, our broken vows, our haunting
sins—which of us is never cast down by a profound sense of failure ? Experience, in the
case of many people, works doubt and dis-
enchantment and disillusion. How shall we
live that happy life in which *experience worketh
hope* ?

The Bible is our great charter of hope. It
confronts the stern and bitter facts of mortal
experience without flinching. But alone among
books it brings us face to face with the Almighty
Helper and Redeemer and Restorer of mankind.
The Bible shows us how God in ages past drew

near to men and chose out a people to become
His witnesses ; how, in the end, He has declared
His will and revealed His redeeming love to the
whole world. In the Bible we discover how the
Divine charity is bearing all things and hoping
all things and believing all things and enduring
all things. And as this love of God is shed
abroad in our hearts, we grow brave with the
only hope that maketh not ashamed—because
it is rooted and grounded in the omnipotence
of everlasting love : and love never faileth.

After a man passes the mid-term of life, he
often grows reluctant to picture what awaits
him in his years to come. One of our modern
poets has imagined a letter written by a young
girl to her own old age. Few of us care to look
so far forward that we see ourselves sitting
wearily by the fire, stretching out withered
hands over the embers. Yet even then—when
everything has happened that is going to happen,
except the greatest event of all—the believer
can lift up his heart in serene, confident expectation. The secret of Christian fortitude
may be put into a nutshell : " He Himself hath
said, I will in no wise fail thee, neither will I
in any wise forsake thee."

There are voices sounding in our ears to-day,
which prophesy evil concerning the cause and
kingdom of Jesus Christ. They declare that the
long slow centuries have at length begun to
prevail against His Church on earth, so that
already it appears decrepit and waxing old and

ready to vanish away. But it remains true
that "Christianity is yet in its infancy,
though it seems, as it has always seemed to
contemporaries, to be in its decay." One
remedy for short-sighted pessimism is to ponder
the history of faith and of faithful souls in all
generations. We have heard with our ears, our
fathers have told us, what noble works God
did in their day and in the old time before them.
We are compassed about with a great cloud of
witnesses. Their Help in ages past is Himself
our Hope for years to come. So when we gaze
into the future, our hearts leap up to behold a
rainbow in the sky.

I AM THE BREAD OF LIFE

THIS saying is a condensed and concentrated
parable. When Christ likened Himself to bread
He took one of those homely illustrations which
He delighted to use. For bread is the simplest,
commonest, and most universal food in the
world. Some plants are limited by climate, or
confined to some special zone of vegetation ;
but corn can grow in nearly every populated
region. Some kinds of food only appeal to an
educated palate : they are caviare to the
general. But we all eat bread, from the
epicure to the starveling ; we find it on every
table and at every meal. Certain sorts of food

can only be had in particular months of the
year ; but bread is never out of season from
January to December. Some dishes and
dainties we can dispense with ; they are costly,
we reserve them for banquets, they furnish the
tables at a feast. But this belongs to the diet
of the masses and the classes alike ; even a
pauper child eats day by day his daily bread.

When our Lord called Himself the Bread of
life He was thinking of the five barley loaves
with which He had fed a hungry crowd the day
before. It was plain fare, some might call it
coarse, though barley bread is still eaten by
peasants all over Europe. But Christ did not
disdain to compare Himself to the simplest and
commonest kind of food. He bids us receive
Him as our prime necessity, as the staff of our
inward life. He calls aloud, not merely to the
noble and the educated, but to a world of hungry
men and women : " Come unto Me, and I will
refresh you."

Herein lies one cardinal difference between
Jesus Christ and other prophets and teachers,
between the Bible and other books. Human
systems and philosophies, framed by art and
man's device, are only fit for superior persons.
They are too fine for humble folk. They make
no provision for the elemental wants of mankind.
They come not to call sinners, but the righteous
—the intellectual aristocracy, the spiritual *élite*.
While for the dim multitude of ordinary men
and women they have no message of hope and

no mission of mercy. Here is the capital defect, the distinctive failure of these ingenious theories of life : they lack the great universal note, they never come home to all sorts and conditions of humanity. It was said that Renan offered the Parisians " *bonbons* flavoured with the infinite " ; and Renan is a type of those religionists who offer us not stones, but rather sweetmeats, instead of bread. But He Whom Christians worship took part in our common flesh and blood. He counted nothing human to be alien from Himself. He was named the Son of Man, because He brought glad tidings to all the poor and the broken-hearted and the captives and the blind. Alone in history He has dared to call Himself the Bread of the whole world.

Again, this phrase not only shows us how simple and catholic the Gospel is, but also points to the conditions on which the Gospel can be received. The natural state which requires food is hunger ; and a healthy man will refuse to eat bread unless it be to satisfy his appetite. Not otherwise is the condition for receiving the Bread which comes down from heaven. Blessed are they that hunger, for they shall be filled. Our inward longing for God carries within itself the pledge of its own satisfaction. If His children ask bread, they can never be finally denied or disappointed. Our restoration, like the prodigal's, generally dates from the day when we begin to be in want. In our Father's house there is always bread enough and to

spare : but we might stay away for ever if sheer
hunger did not mercifully drive us home.

Again, this phrase, the Bread of life, suggests
the assimilation of the Gospel. Bread is no use
to me so long as I only look at it and talk about
it : I must eat it. What doth it profit a hungry
man if you merely explain to him your ideas
about food reform, or tell him how bread ought
to be made, or let him look into a baker's shop-
window ? He must eat, before he can be
strengthened and satisfied. Bread, to nourish
me, must be more even than my property. It
must be taken up into my flesh and blood, so
as to become not only mine but a part of me.

This truth has spiritual applications. The
New Testament, for example, is no use to men
so long as it exists only in a language which they
cannot understand : it must reach them in their
mother-tongue. And even then it is useless,
if it remains unread. Moreover we have to learn
that Jesus Christ Himself profits us nothing, so
long as He is only Some One outside of us and
apart from us. The pages of the New Testament
present Him to our hearts : but we must receive
Him personally and appropriate Him by an act
of faith. Truth, to nourish me, must be made a
living part of my nature. It must be spiritually
assimilated before it can give me spiritual
strength. It must become not only mine, but
me. Even to break the Bread of life to others
is not the same thing as to feed on Him in our
hearts by faith with thanksgiving.

This is one of the mysterious realities which are so difficult in theory, but which become easy and natural in experience. The wisest physiologist cannot perfectly explain by what subtle chemistry physical food is transformed into blood and nerve and muscle ; but this is done daily in the experience of the human race, although not one person in a million so much as thinks about the process. Even so Jesus Christ is made the Bread of life to multitudes of simple souls, who can never explain their experience of that mysterious union which makes them one with His redeeming Love. Nevertheless they feed on the Bread which came down from heaven, and they confess the ineffable fellowship concerning which the apostle said : " I live, yet not I, but Christ liveth in me." Here is a mystery which the poor in spirit enter into, an experience in which the humble are at home. For them the Bread of life becomes the secret of their strength, whereby the inward man is renewed day by day. Because this Divine Gift is not reserved for sacred seasons or set apart for solemn festivals. It is not like the ancient shew-bread which only priests might eat, which common men like David perchance dare taste in some dire necessity. The Bread of life is not too high and good for human nature's daily food. As we live by the faith of the Son of God, we are made partakers of Christ morning by morning, like the manna-gatherers in the desert. Day by day He imparts Himself to the faithful soul : He gives us our daily Bread.

MEASURE FOR MEASURE

THE precept *Give, and it shall be given unto you,* sounds like an ancient proverb—one of those bits of homely wisdom which shrewd folk have coined out of their experience of the world. If the adage be a trifle musty, we recognize that it is true in the main. We admit that one good turn deserves another, and generally secures another in the end. A generous man meets with kindly treatment, while everybody is apt to be churlish with a churl and to act meanly towards a miser. And therefore Mr. Worldly Wiseman and all his tribe accept this doctrine of measure for measure. " He that watereth shall be watered himself." We have plenty of English proverbs to the same effect. " Give an apple where there is an orchard." " Penny wise, pound foolish." " Nothing venture, nothing have." So our Lord's command can be reduced to a maxim of prudential common sense, such as King Solomon might utter and Benjamin Franklin might repeat. Is there anything very original or spiritual in this saying, *Give, and it shall be given unto you ?*

Yet what is originality ? It is not newness : it is rather genuineness. An original teacher says old things with fresh insight and inspiration.

Some of our Lord's precepts may be found scattered among the sentences of the Jewish rabbis. But when He uttered them, men felt that He was not teaching as the scribes. He spake as no man had ever spoken before. And when we ponder it, we discern in this familiar saying a profound principle of the inward life. What seemed a formula of commercial prudence is revealed as an eternal law in the kingdom of heaven. For the spiritual order is not arbitrary. Because it embodies God's character and reflects His will, therefore it knows no variableness. Such laws as " The wages of sin is death " and " The pure in heart shall see God " are part of the nature of things : they fulfil themselves as infallibly as flowers seek the sunlight or the moon swings the sea. What should we say of a herring-boat that took no account of the tides, or of a gardener who tried to rear blossoms in a cavern ? Just so blind and foolish are they who ignore this fundamental truth : *Give, and it shall be given unto you.*

Here is the spiritual rule according to which God deals with His children. We are only able to receive from Him, in proportion as we surrender to Him. *Give, and it shall be given unto you* is the inexorable condition. We read, indeed, of free salvation, without money and without price. We listen to Christ's own words, " Every one that asketh receiveth." Yet these two contrary sayings, " Ask, and it shall be given you," and " Give, and it shall be given you," are just the obverse and reverse of one truth. Because a suppliant, who comes and kneels before his Father, brings his gift with him by that very act. The true penitent who seeks forgiveness must needs have given up already the sin for which he prays to be pardoned. He must have given up his old grudges against the brothers who have injured him ; for only the merciful can obtain mercy. And then a true penitent always brings with him at least the sacrifice of a broken spirit ; and that is the gift which God most desires.

What can we render unto the Lord fit for Him to accept ? We have nothing ; we are worth nothing ; we can offer Him only our own unworthiness, our nothingness, ourselves just as we are. And this is the only offering which He cares to receive. The voice of God is always pleading for this very thing : " Give Me thy heart." Moreover, it must be a gift—and not a bargain. We must not calculate how to make the best of both worlds. Carnal men have dared to offer God a kind of contract—so many alms or prayers or penances, in exchange for so much prosperity. But His love can only be content with a free and willing surrender, such as He Himself makes to us. He demands measure for measure, heart for heart.

By neglecting this condition many go crippled in Christian experience ; their inward life seems to creep on a broken wing. Is not the secret reason why we obtain so little from our God just

Strange legends have clustered round the cup, in history and poetry and fiction. We read of magic goblets, like Joseph's cup by which the Egyptians believed that the interpreter of dreams wrought his divination. We read of enchanted draughts which had baleful potency— like Circe's, which could turn men into beasts, like Siegfried's love-philtre which dazzled his eyes and led his heart astray. We read again of the mysterious elixir of life, one sip of which could give back youth to the aged and quicken vitality in the dying. But when Christ speaks of " My cup," He carries our thoughts far beyond such myths and legends. He points towards His own heart, and bids us contemplate the experience which is hidden there. His promise implies that we shall not merely be brought into His banqueting-house, but that we shall be initiated into His purpose, and have communion with His own thought and feeling, and drink draughts of His very life.

Our Lord's mystic promise to the sons of Zebedee set before them a gift hitherto held back, a blessing kept in store, a grace which they had never tasted yet. In the kingdom of heaven there are divine secrets reserved from the wise and prudent, but revealed to those who are able to receive them. Not every disciple who names Christ's name, and reads His Gospel, and walks in His footsteps, attains to drink of His cup. Not all Christians are counted worthy of so rare a privilege, so high a calling. " Are ye able ? "

the Lord asks wistfully—as though He were to
say : " Ye love Me and follow Me, but your
souls are still dreaming of earthly domination.
Ye seek to reign with Me : but are ye able to
suffer with Me ? " And when they cry confidently, " We are able," He holds out to them
a share in that awful chalice of love and sorrow
and sacrifice, which He drank Himself and where-
of He still grants His best-beloved to drink with
Him.

Something might be said to excuse the request
made by James and John. After all, they were
only asking, as they imagined, that they might
share as closely as possible in their Master's lot.
If He should be enthroned, they begged that they
might sit by His side. Now such a fellowship
in its spiritual aspect is what the Gospel
promises and requires. Pascal has remarked
that it is one of the great principles of Christianity that everything which befell Jesus Christ
must take place also in the soul and the body of
each Christian. Christ died ; and we must be
crucified with Him. He was buried ; and we are
mystically buried with Him. He rose from the
dead ; and we also must walk in newness of life.
He ascended ; and we sit in heavenly places with
Christ Jesus. Everyone who is perfected shall
be even as his Master. Nothing short of this
is involved in a true *imitatio Christi*. It is
impressive to observe how St. Paul sometimes
hints at certain literal resemblances between his
own life and the life of his Lord. " As poor,

yet making many rich," the apostle wrote ;
adding in another place, " though He was rich,
yet for your sakes He became poor." Again
he wrote, " we have no certain dwellingplace,"
" we labour, working with our own hands."
Surely he recollected the Carpenter at Nazareth,
the Pilgrim in Galilee Who had not where to lay
His head. Surely the great apostle felt proud
and thankful, if he could bear in his body any
marks of the Lord Jesus.

> " Yes, let the fragrant scars abide,
>   Love-tokens in Thy stead ;
> Faint shadows of the spear-pierced side,
>   And thorn-encompassed head."

And yet, when Christ speaks of " My cup,"
He suggests far more than any outward correspondence or general imitation. The phrase
carries our thoughts irresistibly to that
experience concerning which He Himself said,
" My soul is exceeding sorrowful, even unto
death," and concerning which He prayed, " If
it be possible, let this cup pass from Me." The
ancient Stoics had declared that a wise and good
man ought never to be troubled : Epictetus had
taught that he should " regard the sins of others
as no evil to himself." But the Son of God
regarded the sins of all men as though they were
His own. The love of the Holiest in contact
with the evil that is in the world—that was the
experience of the Man of Sorrows. And the
New Testament, while it draws us into fellowship
with our Lord, shows us also how He remains

supreme and solitary and separate from sinners.
He endured what we never can suffer, and never
need suffer. His bitter cup was divine and
unfathomable. Alone He has redeemed us
unto God.

Nevertheless this is no empty promise. There
remains a real sense in which His disciples may,
in their measure, indeed drink of Christ's cup.
They attain to it by loving as He loves, by
judging as He judges, by forgiving as He forgives,
by sharing His sympathy with all trouble, by
entering however feebly into His endless compassion which is always being bruised and
acquainted with grief because of unthankful
and evil souls. When we walk at night along
the pavements of any great town, if we had grace
to see the crowds with Christ's eyes and to feel
for them with His pity, we should begin to realize
how sacred and impassioned and awful is this
promise, and how many Christians seem to come
short of it. Concerning this, the proverb is
fulfilled, that there is many a slip 'twixt the cup
and the lip. When the Hussite Reformers in
Bohemia took arms for the right of the laity to
receive the Communion in both kinds, they
marched to battle with a chalice embroidered on
their banner. Yet we may contend valiantly
for Christ's cause, we may prophesy in His name,
we may discuss the meaning of His atonement—
without ever tasting in spirit and in truth the
experience of His heart.

THE Bible exists to show us how God has manifested His Heart and Will to mankind. And, as a consequence and result of God's revelation, the Bible from first to last is calling to its readers in words like these : *O come let us worship*. Moreover the Bible, beyond any other book, makes us feel that a severing gulf is fixed between those who worship and those who worship not. The vital difference in all ages is the difference " between the calculating, smiling, self-contained, self-governed man and the believing, weeping, wondering, struggling, Heaven-governed man, who honours something out of himself and has an amazed sense of a Spiritual Presence, judging, animating, redeeming him." The ninety-fifth Psalm, which is chanted every Sunday morning by millions of Christian worshippers, gives us a clue to some of the essential characteristics of Christian worship.

To begin with, such worship is more than a separate individual act ; it is something corporate and collective. We may quote the comment of a quaint Puritan preacher : " *O come*—there's multitude and concourse ; *let us*—there's unity and concord." Some critics have doubted whether any of the Hebrew Psalms are composed from a personal standpoint ; whether Israel is not always the speaker, even in those passages of confession and aspiration which sound most individualistic. At any rate it is certain that Christians are redeemed from isolation and selfishness into fellowship and brotherhood. The Holy Ghost admits us into the communion of saints. In Christian worship, we unite with the whole family of the faithful, we rejoice in the common salvation, we claim our place and portion in the Israel of God.

Again, in Christian worship we come before God's very presence. For us the way into the holiest has been made open, and we enter the unseen sanctuary. We are brought face to face with the Father and Deliverer of our spirits. In so far as outward forms assist that awful, invisible communion and help our common worship in spirit and in truth, such forms may be justified. But the essence of worship pierces beyond all forms and phrases to that which is within the veil. This is why we must needs draw near with reverence and godly fear—as it is written, *let us kneel before the Lord our Maker*. The methods which men adopt to express their humility and veneration vary with the customs of different races and different ages. For example, a Moslem worshipper while he is reciting his litany will go through a whole elaborate ritual of gesture and assume many distinct attitudes of abasement. In a Russian church Christians as they pray often bow down so low that they touch the stone pavement with their foreheads. In not a few Protestant churches, it is usual to stand or sit during prayer. But the outward attitude of devotion is by comparison of small account : it can avail nothing, unless it be the token of a humble, lowly, penitent, and obedient heart.

The Psalm reminds us, again, that our normal Christian worship should be pitched in the key of praise and exultation. Too often we let the *Miserere* overpower the *Jubilate* and the *Magnificat* and the *Gloria in excelsis*. But the ideal worship of the faithful is a great thanksgiving for God's unspeakable gift in the redemption of all mankind.

Then this Psalm suggests one further element in Christian worship, which we lose sight of too often. No passage of Holy Scripture is more entirely penetrated with the wonder and glory of the world which God has made. The Hebrew singer appeals to the strength of the hills and the music of the waves, as though he heard those two great voices, one of the sea and one of the mountains, which our English poet heard proclaiming the same mysterious message. But the Psalm goes on to speak of yet another Voice, far more profound and awful than the harmonies of nature, the Voice which is never silent—of the Shepherd, the Deliverer, the King of men. *To-day if ye will hear His voice, harden not your hearts.* Our worship is incomplete, unless beyond our common praises and confessions and petitions, we listen together to hear what God the Lord shall say. For He is speaking daily to the heart of every man. And often He speaks most clearly when our hearts are melted and subdued in the unity of Christian worship. It has been pointed out that the word " obedience " is by derivation akin to the word " audience." The obedient soul is the listening soul. Concerning Christ Himself it is written that He was obedient unto death : " from the first to the last our Lord was listening, always listening for the still, small voice of God." And Christian worship has this for its issue and consummation, that therein we hear God's call and respond to God's claim.

The visions of heaven in the New Testament set before us a continuance of worship which we have begun on earth. Such a picture may seem dreary and monotonous to those who have never learnt how Christian worship rises to its climax in adoration. In the doxology which ends the Lord's Prayer we are bidden to say, " Thine is the kingdom and the power and the glory." For it is man's bondage and misery to be under the curse of self-willing, self-seeking, self-glorying—to have no object of delight and worship but himself. We are redeemed from that curse, as our spirits see themselves and lose themselves in Him Who is Light, and in Whom is no darkness at all—Who is Love, and in Whom there is no selfishness at all. Our worship passes into pure adoration. It arises out of the needs of sinful, suffering creatures here, but it can grow into the rapture of the spirits of just men made perfect before the throne of God.

GOD'S FELLOW-WORKERS

IN the Bible as a rule work means agriculture —the husbandry of the plough-share and the pruning-hook. Ever since Adam lost the keeping of the garden, his sons in exile have had for their chief task the tilling of the ground. And this most primitive form of labour is still the most necessary—whereby man wins his bread out of the dust of which he was made. St. Paul has agriculture in mind when he describes himself and other Christian teachers as labourers side by side in the field and garden of God. But the apostle says more. In this common toil we are fellow-workers with God Himself. We work for Him and under Him, but we also work with Him. Our effort, our patience, our success are bound up with His own.

There are weird medieval legends of men, like Faust, who had entered into partnership with the powers of evil. They let the unholy spirit possess and control them. They became fellow-workers together with Satan. People who have only a shallow experience of what is possible in the human soul scoff at tales of black art— as though such legends did not stand for a dreadful reality. At any rate it is gloriously

possible to go into partnership with the Power
of goodness. We may yield ourselves to be
possessed and controlled by the Holy Spirit.
We may become fellow-workers together with
God. We may know the perpetual indwelling
of Him Who governs our desires and purifies
our hopes and sustains our efforts and retrieves
our failures.

From its first trial to its last triumph the
Christian life is one long co-operation with
Christ. We do not redeem ourselves, or convert
ourselves, or sanctify ourselves. Alike in the act
of repentance and in the venture of faith, we
are fellow-workers with God. He alone makes
us able to trust ourselves to Him. We could
never say " Lord, I believe," unless the Lord
were helping our unbelief, prompting and
inspiring the reluctant soul to launch out upon
His everlasting arms. The love of Christ constrains us into each fresh consecration, each new
surrender. And so the holiest Christian will
always confess " By the grace of God I am what
I am. At best I am only a feeble co-operator
in His purpose and His patience towards me."

Spiritual experience derives not merely its
earliest impulse from God, but along every
point of its path it is carried by heavenly attraction and swayed by Divine control. Even in
those moods and acts of the inward man which
appear most individual and self-originated, we
are no more than workers together with our
Redeemer. For example, in the duty of self-

examination I must fail utterly, if I am merely my own examiner. I deceive myself instinctively, I flatter myself unawares, unless I can turn to the Searcher of hearts and cry : " Search me, and know my heart : try me and know my thoughts : and see if there be any wicked way in me, and lead me in the way everlasting." So again, in the duty of self-discipline I could never train and temper my own spirit if I had not within me One Who is Himself the Director of my soul. I could never curb my own wilfulness, if I had not One Who is the Governor of my will—Who besets me behind and before and lays His hand upon me, to humble me and to prove me and to make me poor in spirit and pure in heart. The task of self-culture would be hopeless, we should despair of the spiritual fabric unless it had a Divine Architect, unless we could say concerning the house of character that its builder and maker is God.

In the work of faith and the labour of love and the patience of hope we are God's fellow-workers. And this alone gives us leave to hope to the end. The guarantee of final perseverance is that He Who has begun a good work in us shall surely finish it. For " it is not God's way to do things by halves." The pledge consists not in our fidelity or sincerity, but in the Name of Him Who is Faithful and True.

Moreover, in our practical activity we are also God's fellow-workers. This applies even to the drudgery of everyday duty. Each honest

labourer on earth is carrying out a fragment of
the Divine plan. Whoever produces or distri-
butes things useful or things beautiful is helping
on the good work of the world. To drain the
fen, to plough the prairie, to build the cottage,
to weave the cloth, to cook the meal, to nurse
the sick, to play with the children—is to co-
operate with God's great purpose. And when
we try, as we say, "to do good," we ought to
feel ourselves in a special sense the agents and
instruments of His will. On this point Bishop
Creighton left two pregnant maxims : "Nothing does good to others except what comes out
of our own experience." "The only way in
which we can help others is by recalling the
way in which God has dealt with ourselves."
Nor dare we forget that the Eternal Teacher
is dealing with those whom we desire to teach
and to bless. Our best words can only say
"Amen" to the lessons of the Holy Ghost.
When we visit the mourners in some desolate
home, the Comforter Himself is there already.
When we seek for those who have gone astray,
the Good Shepherd is out in the wilderness
before us. Alas! that too often we ignore His
co-operation. We think and act and speak
as though He were not always working in all
souls, even in the most evil and thankless souls
alive.

Surely when we provide men of all kindreds
and nations and tongues with the New Testament, we become in a most profound and prac-

tical sense God's fellow-workers. For we are helping, in our measure, to carry out the express purpose of His revelation of Himself to the world. We are bringing home to strangers and foreigners the good news that they are not forgotten or deserted, but loved with everlasting love and redeemed by Divine sacrifice— the good news that God has taken the burden of humanity upon His own Heart. The cure of all souls is His peculiar charge. We are less than the least of His fellow-workers; in His hands are we and our words and our works. And the universe will not finally disappoint Him Who has made it, Who is remaking it day by day. Those who are God's fellow-workers shall enter at last into the joy of God's victory.

WHY ART THOU CAST DOWN?

THE characteristic feature about the Psalms, which makes them so dear to every generation of sinful and sorrowful men, is their deep, vivid, pervading sense of the relation between the soul and God. All through the Psalter the fact of such a relation—direct and close and immediate—is taken for granted. To us Christians the nearness of God, and His personal affection, and His familiar friendship, have become axioms of faith. But these were strange,

new truths which entered the world when the
Psalms were born. To primitive men God
seemed mighty indeed, and awful, and supreme ;
yet so far as each individual was concerned,
God was always aloof and far away. When
we read fragments of the poetry of early religions, we marvel at the lofty thoughts which
breathe in the ancient hymns of India or
Greece. But we discover this profound note of
difference between such hymns and the Hebrew
Psalter. They are voices of men yearning after
an absent, nameless deity, seeking after a God
whom they feel to be a great way off. Whereas
the Psalms (as Dean Church puts it) are the
voice of a man who has found God for himself,
who possesses God for his own. His soul has
secret access, everywhere and every moment,
to the Infinite Compassion, the Eternal and All-
sufficing Goodness. To God, as into the heart
of the tenderest of friends, he can pour out his
distresses. Before God, as at the feet of a faithful comforter and guide, he can lay down the
burden of his care. Through every variety of
experience, in passionate longing, in sorrowful
reproach, in bitter bereavement, in eager
wistful hope, the Psalms express what God is
to the soul.

Here, for example, in Psalms xlii and xliii,
which were perhaps originally one, we listen to
a colloquy between the singer and his own soul
and God. We hear the words of his desire and
his complaint, of his despair and his confidence,

calling and answering each other like the murmur of those waves and billows which they mention. And then, in thrice-repeated refrain, the Psalmist turns pathetically and rebukes and chides his soul for its own impatience and despondency. *Why art thou cast down, O my soul? and why art thou disquieted within me? Hope thou in God, for I shall yet praise Him, who is the health of my countenance, and my God.*

We fail to enter into the Psalter until we have realized this first and last truth of the union between the creature and the Creator, the human soul and its Heavenly Friend. Perhaps we must endure some of the trials, we must wade through the deep waters and dark nights, which the Psalms describe, before we attain to that abiding, overwhelming sense of God which inspires them all. For it is in supreme hours of solitude and anguish that God draws near and reveals Himself to our spirits. We are led to understand the nothingness of things around us, and we begin by degrees to perceive that there are but two beings in the whole universe—our own soul and the God Who made it. We become conscious that we are alone with the Eternal, and like the Psalmist we find in Him our refuge from the perplexities and calamities of life. " I am continually with Thee : Thou hast holden me by Thy right hand. Thou shalt guide me with Thy counsel, and afterward receive me to glory. My flesh and my heart faileth : but God is the strength of my

10

heart, and my portion for ever. Thou wilt show me the path of life : in Thy presence is the fulness of joy. When I awake up after Thy likeness I shall be satisfied with it."

Why art thou cast down, O struggling soul ? Dost thou go mourning all the day long because of the oppression of the enemy ? Is it because of the daily battle with the world and the evil one, because when the spirit is willing the flesh is weak ? Hope thou in God. He Who has made thee remembers that thou art dust. He will not suffer thee to be tried above what thou art able to bear. He cannot forsake the work of His own hands.

Why art thou cast down, O faltering soul ? Art thou dismayed by thine own doubts and fears ? Canst thou win no certainty amid these shadows and confusions, no quietness from the strife of tongues ? Hope thou in God. If thy heart misgive thee, He is greater than thy heart and surer than thy faith. And thou shalt yet praise Him, in the land where all doubts are strangers.

Why art thou cast down, O solitary soul ? Is it by reason of disappointment and desertion and betrayal ? Hope thou in the One Friend Who is entirely faithful, the One Love Who was never yet found less than true. His purpose for thee is far more wonderful than thy self-planning. When all others fail and forsake thee, He shall clasp thee the closer in everlasting arms.

Why art thou cast down, O loyal soul ?

Because thy labour goes unrecompensed and thy sacrifice unnoticed, and thy patience unpraised ? Because after these many years men call thy service foolishness and thy life a failure ? Hope thou in God, for His voice is whispering " Thou art My beloved . . . I am thy exceeding great reward."

The patience of hope can chant this song before sunrise : *I shall yet praise Him.* Heart answers to heart across the centuries. The Hebrew poet feels, what we sometimes feel, that he cannot honestly thank God for troubles while he is still in the thick of them. He can only trust dumbly in the dark, and watch the eastern sky for the morning star. He can only bow his head and let the storm sweep over him. He is anchored on the Rock, but he has no voice, no spirit left for hallelujahs at present. His faith and hope are holding out, but they are hardly triumphant. He cannot glory in tribulations yet : perhaps he falls as far short of St. Paul's great rapture as we do. But how honest he is, how simple and sincere ! We have all heard prayers and sermons spoiled by the fatal falsetto note. We have all attended religious meetings where the rhetoric rang hollow and the fervour was exaggerated. But, while we confess that Christ reigns, it is right to add humbly, " We see not yet all things put under Him." We shall see it, some day—but to-day we walk by faith, not by sight.

Most of all, in our own prayers we are bound

to be utterly honest, to speak the simple truth.
The Psalmist is a pattern of sad sincerity.
" I shall praise God after awhile," he says,
" but just now I can do no more than hold on to
Him, with all my heart and soul and strength.
He has not taught me all the secret, nor wiped
away all the tears.   Why He deals thus with me,
I cannot tell. But it must be right ; and some
day He will make it bright. Doubtless God will
make me thankful at last for every step of the
road He is leading me, thankful for every
drop in the cup He is giving me to drink.   I
can submit to it all now, and I believe that
I shall be glad about it all in the end.

" My losses, my disappointments, my lonely
hours—I shall be thankful to my God for
every one of them at last. I shall yet praise Him
because He fastened me to the cross which
crucified my selfishness. I shall yet praise Him
for all those waves and billows which helped
to drown my pride.   I shall yet praise Him
because He made my plans frustrate, and denied
my dearest ambition, so that He might subdue
me to His own holy and perfect will. I shall yet
praise Him for the weakness which wrecked
me on His everlasting strength.   I shall yet
praise Him because He took away my treasures,
and removed lover and friend far from my side,
and set me in a solitary place, so that in emptiness and desolation He might make Himself
more than all to my soul.   I shall yet praise
Him, because though I be deserted and broken

down and sick at heart, I know now as I never knew before that God Himself is my portion for ever. O God, Thou art my God. When I see Thee as Thou art, I'll praise Thee as I ought. Whom have I in heaven but Thee ? and there is none upon earth that I desire beside Thee."

MORE FOR GOD

FEW Christians can read without emotion the story of Francis Xavier, the young Spanish nobleman, who gave up home and friends and country and all that makes life dear, that he might declare among the heathen the unsearchable riches of Christ. Xavier was one of the seven men who bound themselves by a common vow of pilgrimage and service, and thus began what grew into the famous Society of Jesus. To-day the word Jesuit, derived originally from the Name which is above every name, has sunk into a term of reproach. Yet the darkest pages in Jesuit history need not blind us to the devotion out of which that history sprang. Not long after the order had been established, Xavier was chosen by his superior for a mission to the East Indies. When he heard of his vocation, he confessed that he had long cherished a secret desire to labour in those far-distant lands. God, he said, had already revealed to him what great things he must suffer there for his Master's sake. There passed before his eyes as he slept a vision of stormy seas and barren shores and barbarous peoples, a promise of toil and hunger and peril and persecution. And when he beheld this picture of his own coming trials, he was so transported by the thought of being counted worthy to suffer for Christ that he cried out fervently in the Latin which was the mother-tongue of his prayers : *Amplius, Domine, amplius*—that is to say, " Yet more, O Lord, yet more : give me more to endure, more to undergo, more to overcome."

Such was the fiery watchword of Xavier's life—a life which, for all its superstition and fanaticism, bears the marks of an apostle. In ten short years he had gathered converts in Goa, in Travancore, in Malaya, and in Japan, dying at last on the coast of China where also he longed to carry the Gospel. Let us allow that his success has been exaggerated, that his doctrine was clouded with errors, that the very missions he founded perished through the corruption of those who came after him, that the Society for which he lived and died has proved a curse rather than a blessing to the world. And yet Francis Xavier himself, with his quenchless zeal, his tireless energy, his boundless sacrifice, his eager ambition to spend and be spent for God—this great missionary came nearer than some of his critics to St. Paul's own example, just as his passionate prayer sounds like an echo of St. Paul's words : " We beseech you, brethren, and exhort you by

the Lord Jesus, that ye abound more and
more."

Of all mortal contradictions and absurdities
the most dreadful is a self-complacent Christian.
In this world, indeed, no man can be really
satisfied unless he is torpid, which means only
half alive. Why, every other person we meet
in the market-place has *amplius* written on his
forehead. He is toiling and scheming and
saving to get more, to pile more goods into the
warehouse, to rake more gold into the bank.
And as it is in trade, so it is in art and learning
and ambition. Each goal becomes a fresh
starting-point, each prize acts like a new spur.
And though this deep human instinct over-
reaches itself, yet it remains after all a royal
quality, which could hardly belong to creatures
who were mere slaves of space and time. When
a little child stretches out his hands to claim
everything he sees, he is like an unconscious
prophet of his own possibilities. The child is
father of the man, and the true man is always
" a man of desires "—unsatisfied with his best
success, and after his grandest victories weeping
for fresh worlds to conquer.

A self-contented Christian is hardly a Christian at all. *Amplius* is the true saint's watchword. If we are taught by the Holy Ghost,
each inward lesson makes us athirst for purer
knowledge. If we grow stronger against selfishness, each conquered and crucified sin makes us
eager for a more complete victory. If we gain

a glimpse of the King in His beauty, we are kindled with the hope which Tennyson confessed was his supreme ambition—the hope of a clearer vision of God. Looking back across the years, we can give thanks for wonderful experiences of the Divine love and mercy. When we close the book of memory, we must write *Great Benedictions* on the last page as a colophon. But by that very token we are bold to write *Great Expectations* across the cover of the sealed volume of our future.

The supreme need of our souls is to pray *Amplius, Domine, amplius*.

> " O the little more, and how much it is ;
> And the little less, and what worlds away ! "

" A little more of absolute surrender ; a little more of childlike trust ; a little more of tenderness of conscience ; a little more of venturing faith and unquestioning obedience, and how much it would mean for ourselves and for the world." Then the darkness would pass and the true light shine again. Then, going forth weeping, bearing precious seed, with hearts softened and strengthened by penitence, we should come again rejoicing, bringing our sheaves with us.

When we come into the presence of the Crucified, we who are Christ's can have only one hope, one wish, one prayer : " *Amplius, Domine, amplius*. More from Thee, O Lord, and more for Thee. Is there aught that such

as Thou canst take from such as I ? Are my
hands worthy of Thy service ? Can my heart
enter into Thy Passion ? Show me anything
to bear or to dare for Thy sake. Show me more,
O Lord, show me more ! " This was the spirit
of Xavier's prayer. He was not asking for
personal gifts or selfish blessings. He was
pleading for a larger share in the Divine burden,
and wider opportunities for service and sacrifice,
and a fuller portion in the fellowship of the
sufferings of Christ.

The Church as a whole has never quite lost
the instinct of its world-wide mission. There
is no surer apostolic note than this imperious
sense of a charge only half-fulfilled. The
missionary prayer of the faithful must always
be *Amplius, Domine, amplius*—making every
success the stepping-stone for new effort, and
pressing forward to complete the illimitable
task which Christ bequeathed to His disciples
when He bade them begin to conquer the world
in His Name. Perhaps one chief earthly reward
of devotion to this mission comes in a more
absorbing and constraining sense of its unspeakable claim. Those Christians who have given
themselves up to it most unreservedly in the
past cry with fresh ardour as they gaze upward
and onward—*Amplius, Domine, amplius*.

It has been said that the Advent of Jesus Christ altered the moral axis of the world. And when we speak of His Advent, we use that word to embrace the whole series of events which began with the Nativity and which came to their climax in the Passion and Resurrection and Ascension. In a real sense Easter only fulfils the implicit promise of Christmas. The Lord's humiliation leads up to the Lord's exaltation. When He took it upon Him to deliver man, He overcame the sharpness of death, He opened the kingdom of heaven to all believers. Everything has become different since the Church first learned to sing that strange new song : *Now is Christ risen from the dead*.

Even to our Lord Himself we may reverently suppose that Easter in retrospect must needs be unlike Easter in prospect. In the days of His flesh the Redeemer foresaw not only His Cross but His glorious triumph over the power of death. He warned His unheeding disciples that He must needs suffer many things, and be crucified, and rise again. Step by step His prophecy came to pass, until He could say concerning the whole, *It is finished*. A profound Christian thinker has ventured to imagine what it will be like for any of us hereafter to look back upon our own dying as an experience

left behind : " to be past death—to have
accomplished that one amazing act which we
have yet undone before us, and are to do, to
know what that awful and mysterious thing is,
and that its pains and terrors are gone past
for ever." Some hint of a kindred thought
gives weight to the Apostle's words : *Christ
being raised from the dead, dieth no more : death
hath no more dominion over Him.*

Most impressive and significant is the fact
that every book of the New Testament is dated
" after Easter." That is to say, it is all written
by authors who live and move and have their
being in the radiant sunlight of Christ's resurrection. They have recorded whatever we know
about the historic Jesus, but they write as men
who are already in fellowship with the risen
Christ. To quote a modern apologist, " Faith
in the resurrection was not only prevalent, but
immensely powerful before any of our New
Testament books were written. Not one of
them would have been written but for that
faith. It is not this or that in the New Testament—it is not the story of the empty tomb,
or of the appearing of Jesus in Jerusalem or in
Galilee—which is the primary evidence of the
resurrection ; it is the New Testament itself.
The life that throbs in it from beginning to end,
the life that always fills us again with wonder
as it beats upon us from its pages, is the life
which the risen Saviour has quickened in
Christian souls. . . . The existence of the

Christian Church, the evidence of the New
Testament : these incomparable phenomena in
human history are left without adequate or
convincing explanation if the resurrection of
Jesus be denied." We should never have had
any New Testament if the creed had ended—as
some people think a Christian creed might end
—with "crucified, dead, and buried." In a
sense, the Gospels and Acts and Epistles themselves fulfil the Lord's promise : *Because I live,
ye shall live also.*

The full Christian experience can only be
realized by men and women who learn the
spiritual meaning of " after Easter." The late
Dr. Dale recorded how he was once writing an
Easter sermon, and when half-way through,
the thought of the risen Lord broke in upon
him as it had never done before. " ' Christ is
alive,' I said to myself. ' Alive ! ' And then
I paused. ' Alive ! ' and then I paused again.
' Alive ! ' Can that really be true ? Living as
really as I myself am ? I got up and walked
about repeating, ' Christ is living ! Christ is
living ! ' At first it seemed strange and hardly
true, but at last it came upon me as a burst of
sudden glory. Yes, Christ is living. It was to
me a new discovery. I thought that all along
I had believed it, but not until that moment
did I feel sure about it."

We are not Christians merely because we
read the evangelists with the sentimental
realism with which we might read some historical

novel, and then try to reproduce in imagination the figure of One Who thus toiled and taught and suffered in Syria so many centuries ago. That is not enough. " It is not because He lived, but because He lives, that we have life also." The New Testament writers never think of Christ as belonging to a bygone past. To them He is the Beginning and the End, the First and the Last, and the Living One—alive for evermore. The resurrection translated Him into our actual present, with all the grace of His earthly living and dying, with all His omnipotence to heal and forgive and save. To those who are children of His resurrection He communicates the energies of the world to come. They walk henceforth not by the law of a carnal commandment, but by the power of His endless life.

THE TREASURE OF THE HUMBLE

WHEN we observe it in other people's characters, pride is a vice which we instinctively resent and condemn. Yet there is no quality which we are so apt to excuse and tolerate in ourselves. Self-assertion and self-glorification appear detestable in our neighbours ; but in our own case they seem only a part of manly self-respect. The Gospel, however, shatters our complacency, and brings down our conceit into the dust. It

demands first and foremost that we become poor
in spirit. It can never be received or even
understood by self-satisfied persons : but the
humble shall hear thereof and be glad.

Now to be humble does not mean simply that
you submit to superior authority, or that you
recognize your own puny place in the boundless
creation of God. Teachers like Carlyle have
rebuked human vanity by pointing to the
midnight sky—that majestical roof fretted with
golden fire—where the stars which were shining
before the first man drew breath will endure
after the last man has vanished away. But
humility in the Christian sense of the word is
something far more profound and passionate.
It is not generally produced by some abstract
idea of holiness or by the rigour of a righteous
law. Humility is the effect of personal contact
with some holy person ; above all, it results
from the heart-piercing sense of unworthiness
which is created in us when we come face to
face with Jesus Christ. The New Testament
explains it in a single sentence : " When I saw
Him, I fell at His feet as dead."

The beatitudes of the Sermon on the Mount
describe different aspects of the treasure of the
humble. Our Lord pronounces His benediction
upon those who know themselves bankrupt and
beggared of goodness ; those who are broken
down from self-sufficiency, and broken in from
self-will ; those who are hungry and thirsty
after holiness which they have never attained ;

those who are endlessly pitiful, because they feel how utterly they themselves need day by day to be forgiven. These beatitudes mark the eternal difference which there is in the sight of God between " the calculating, smiling, self-contained, self-governed man, and the be-lieving, weeping, wondering, struggling, Heaven-governed man, who honours something outside of himself, and has an amazed sense of a Spiritual Presence guiding, animating, redeem-ing him."

We all admit that the Christian life begins in humility. The contrite sinner's voice always utters one prayer : " God be merciful to me, a sinner." We do not always realize that Chris-tian experience must go on, and continue to the end, in the spirit and temper of the same prayer. In man's pilgrimage through the wilderness the Divine aim is this : " to humble thee, and to prove thee, and to know what is in thy heart." Our spiritual attainment is measured by humility, which persists and deepens year after year.

Now in a special sense Holy Scripture is the treasure of the humble. Unless he has this inward qualification, the most learned student will be sure to wander and miss the track. For the Bible filleth the hungry with good things ; but the rich it sends empty away. None except the poor in spirit are able to read God's Book from within. But for them the seals of revelation have been broken, and they move among the mysteries of the New Testament like children at home in their Father's house.

No Christian grace is more precious than humility, or more potent for the highest good. There is something strange and wonderful about the influence wielded by any man who is genuinely humble in heart. It seems as if God can afford to grant popularity and applause to a soul that has risen above things like these, and renounced them, and disdained them. God can entrust the outward and visible tokens of success to a soul that knows how to reckon such tokens at their proper worth. To a man of this rare type, people cannot help yielding the very crown which he is content to forgo. So the humble, unworldly Christian wakes up with surprise, almost with amusement, to find the world about him at his feet.

Nevertheless, to the saints on earth spiritual pride remains their subtlest temptation. Because humility, by its very nature, vanishes if it so much as becomes aware of itself. No man clothed with humility can grow conscious of the heavenly raiment he wears. Moreover the busiest and most successful Christians are often most sorely tempted into self-flattery and self-esteem. He Who knows what is in man warns us sternly against the peril of this snare. A wise modern teacher has thus paraphrased our Lord's warning : " Performance of duty is no merit. Do faithfully and punctiliously all that God commands thee to do ; and, having achieved that which thou well knowest none save thyself has ever achieved, thou art nevertheless an unprofitable servant. Thou hast not exceeded thy duty. Nay, if thou indeed believe that thou hast performed thy whole duty, thou art judged already ; for thou hast judged thyself."

It was in this spirit that the author of *Rock of Ages* described his hymn as " a living and dying prayer for the holiest believer in the world." Above William Carey's grave are written words dear to humble souls in the hour of death :

> " A guilty, weak and helpless worm,
>   On Thy kind arms I fall.
> Be Thou my strength and righteousness,
>   My Jesus, and my all."

BUT YE SEE ME

WHEN the Son of Man came to the evening of His mortal life, He parted with His disciples at a feast. The hour was at hand when the Bridegroom should be taken away from them ; but He comforted their grief with the promise that His absence would be only apparent. " Yet a little while and the world seeth Me no more ; *but ye see Me.*" Though He be visible no longer to their bodily eyes, He will not leave them comfortless. He will come and make His abode in their spirits by His own Spirit. He will possess them with His eternal presence. He Himself will dwell as a living Person in their hearts.

Through the tumult and conflict of generations Christ keeps His parting promise. Amid dim lights and tangled circumstance Christians still prove by experience how surely He manifests Himself to His disciples as He doth not unto the world. It was outside Jericho, on His last journey, that a blind beggar arrested Him with passionate cries for mercy. And when the Lord asked, " What wilt thou ? " the man answered (according to one ancient Syriac manuscript of the Gospels), " Lord, that Thou wouldst open my eyes, *that I may see Thee.*" That primitive gloss sums up the very gist of the blessing which we inherit. To-day, in our perplexed and sorrowful confusions, what Christians need is not general illumination, but the vision of the Lord's own countenance ; not knowledge to understand all mysteries, but the light of the knowledge of God's glory in the face of Jesus Christ.

Though He has ascended into heaven, our Lord has left behind Him on earth two legacies —the Bible and the Church, concerning each of which His words come true : " ye see Me." In Scripture there are, as St. Peter confessed, some things hard to be understood. But Scripture, taken as a whole, sets its face unmistakably towards one supreme Object. Sacred history moves upward to a climax, and culminates in the Person of the Redeemer. There are some devout interpreters who indulge in expositions of both Testaments which often seem fanciful, even fantastic. A sober student will revolt against their mystical conceits, their elaborate allegorizing of Jewish types and antitypes. Yet after all, if men have gone astray when they sought to discern Christ in every verse of the Bible, their error is as nothing compared with the blindness which can recognize in its record no Divine Saviour, and discover there no revelation of the mystery of God.

For us who are Christ's it is not quite easy to consider questions of Biblical criticism with an unbiased mind. We admit our Christian duty to welcome fresh truth, from whatever source it may reach us. But we are certified already as to the deepest and surest truths of our own inward experience. We may be in doubt as to the meaning and value of many parts of Scripture; but in the pages of this Book we have met and recognized and worshipped the Lord and Lover of our souls. We may even feel less certain about His miracles in Galilee than we feel about the healing which Christ has wrought in our own characters; and so we cannot help approaching controversies as to the Gospel records with a settled faith in His power, His grace, and His glory. We know for ourselves that He is the Saviour of men; for we have received through Him the remission of our sins, and He has translated us into His own kingdom of righteousness and peace and joy.

Moreover, this same principle applies to the Church as well as to the Bible. Ecclesiastical history includes many stained and chequered chapters. We must confess, for example, that the persecutions of Christians by pagans have been far less cruel and terrible than the persecutions carried on by Christians against one another. In these days nothing is so easy and so cheap, nothing is so popular, as to point a scornful finger at the corruptions and divisions and failures in modern Christendom. Nevertheless, amid all the Church's failures, we who are Christ's can recognize also something grander and holier and more wonderful, something which is not of this world. We have met with men and women who have been transformed into living epistles and gospels. We have seen Jesus Christ Himself, realized and revealed afresh in the lineaments of those who love Him. So long as the Church produces saints, as it certainly does—so long as the love of Christ appears visibly working in Christian lives and characters—the Church is indestructible and eternal : the tabernacle of God is with men.

In the pages of the Gospel, in the fellowship of the Church, Christ still says to His disciples, " But ye see Me." There are seasons and moods when our Christian worship appears stale and unprofitable. Sometimes the ritual may seem superstitious ; sometimes the prayers may sound mechanical ; sometimes the sermon may sink into vulgar rhetoric or scholastic reasoning. Yet whenever a handful of humble believers gather together to adore their Redeemer, He manifests Himself in their midst. They realize His spiritual Presence, closer than breathing, nearer than hands and feet. To-day, as of old, He makes Himself our living Bread, and our true Vine, and our everlasting Rest.

THE LORD SHALL REJOICE IN HIS WORKS

THE Bible never speaks about " Nature." In Hebrew there is no word which corresponds to such an idea. Faithful men of old could not conceive of the universe as existing apart and abstracted from God. By His word He called all things into being, and moment by moment He controls them by His power, He sustains them by His will. In Psalm civ, for example, creation throbs and overflows with the passionate life of the Creator. And as often as spring awakens and May-time comes round once more, we can enter afresh into the exultation of the Psalmist. For a smile has crept back over the face of the earth. " The grass grows bright, the boughs are swollen with blooms. Above, birds fly in merry flocks, the lark soars up and up, shivering for very joy. Savage creatures seek their loves in wood and plain—and God renews His ancient rapture."

Even with regard to human efforts, it is true, as Ruskin insisted, that work does not deserve to be called good, in the doing of which the craftsman himself has taken no pleasure and found no satisfaction. When we study a genius like Shakespeare, for example, we can feel that he must have written with immense exuberance and enjoyment. So when we meditate humbly on the wondrous works of God, we begin to understand that they not only declare His glory but also bear witness to His infinite happiness. If little children can delight in daisy-chains, it is not irreverent to say that God must take pure delight in daisies—else why does He go on making them by millions? The flowers and the stars, the ants and the angels, are alike the work of His fingers. " The glory of the Lord shall endure for ever : the Lord shall rejoice in His works."

The Psalmist, indeed, does not shut his eyes to the stern and dreadful aspects of creation. He has courage to sing : " Thou makest darkness, and it is night." To his faith, storm and earthquake and hunger and pain and death are equally " acts of God "—the same God who is righteous in all His ways and holy in all His works. William Blake's poem on " The Tiger " puts in poignant form a question which has no answer :

" Did He smile His work to see ?
Did He, Who made the lamb, make thee ? "

The Bible does not explain the strange and terrible contradiction. In this life at least, human minds can never fully resolve it. We have no skill to unravel the tangled threads of suffering which are woven into the whole texture of the world. Such knowledge is too wonderful for us : it is high, we cannot attain unto it. We can only bow our heads and worship the mystery of God's will, and believe that His tender mercies are over all His works, in all places of His dominion.

But further, it seems as though the All Merciful and Almighty had chosen to limit His dominion, or rather, to share it with the beings whom He has created. For He has trusted human creatures with strange and terrible power to corrupt and pervert and destroy His original handiwork. Often, for instance, we quote Cowper's hackneyed line : " God made the country, and man made the town." Yes, man made the slums and the gambling-dens and the slave-markets and the battle-fields. Perhaps, if we could see things with God's eyes and measure by the judgment of eternity, the streets of a great city at night would appear a more appalling spectacle than any battle-field. When we realize even a little of what man has made of man, dare we believe that the Lord rejoices in *our* works ?

Turning back to the Bible, we learn what is the most mighty and mysterious among all the works of God. The Gospel reveals His supreme act of redemption and reparation, of reversal and retrieval. For man's sake the Divine Love enters into the evil and misery which man has created, and endures its burden, and conquers its curse, and bears away the sin of the world. In the New Testament we discover how the manger declares the glory of God, and the Cross showeth His handiwork. There, with His own right hand and with His holy arm, the Lord hath wrought salvation for us. Every Christian will confess, " Thou, Lord, hast made me glad through Thy work." Our faith rejoices in what has been done for us, once for all. And surely He also, who is the Author and Finisher of faith, must exult in what He Himself has accomplished. So far as we dare speak of it in mortal language, we may say that even in the depths of the Divine Sacrifice there dwells a secret and awful joy. Already His affliction worketh a far more exceeding and eternal weight of glory. We see not yet all things put under Him. We dare not say to-day that the Lord rejoices even in His Church. But we know that at last He shall see of His travail, and shall be satisfied. In the end it shall be as it was in the beginning—when God saw all His work, and behold it was very good.

LIFT UP YOUR EYES ON HIGH

ON the brink of each new year men pause for a breathing space, so that they may look

backward and look forward. To-day the retrospect and the prospect alike are tempting
multitudes of persons into dejection, if not into
dismay. When the war ended, we faced the
future with such eager hopes for England and
for the world. But we have lived since then
through so many illusions, we have tasted so
many disappointments. Serious and thought-
ful people, indeed, are not carried away by wild
hysterical talk about our civilization falling to
pieces. The fabric of society which in God's
providence has been built up through long
generations will not collapse into red ruin in a
night. Nevertheless the outlook is tragic and
menacing enough to excuse gloomy prophets.
Even good men's hearts often fail them for
fear, as they listen to the sea and the waves
roaring. Most Christians are profoundly conscious of weariness and disappointment. Sometimes they fall into the mood of the old monk
who chanted *Hora novissima, tempora pessima*,
as he gazed through the bars of his cloister at
Clugny and saw a world full of evil and misery.

Lift up your eyes on high. A gifted commentator points out how that message came to
Israel in captivity on the vast Babylonian
plain. There the exiles had been trampled
into servitude, their very language was being
stifled in Babel, their patriotism was crushed
into the tyrant's mud and mortar. Yet high
above the desperate flatness, the deadening
crowd, God's stars were shining in the dark

sky : and it was upon the steadfast stars that the prophet bade his people fix their eyes and feed their hearts. *He gathereth the outcasts of Israel . . . He telleth the number of the stars . . . He calleth them all by name ; by the greatness of His might, and for that He is strong in power, not one is lacking.* They are symbols of the unfailing grace of God, the assurance of His will to redeem and to restore.

There is a wise saying of Henry Drummond's : " When the outlook is bad, try the up-look." The art of life consists in paying attention to the right things, the things which seriously matter, and neglecting the rest. Now the things which matter most of all are those spiritual realities which we can never discern until we obey the bidding of the ancient prophet : *Lift up your eyes on high.*

Many years ago the present writer climbed with a friend before daybreak on to the roof of Milan Cathedral, to watch the sunrise. Standing among the marble spires, they had a dull, dreary prospect. Northward spread the immense plain of Lombardy, all veiled and shrouded in mists ; and as twilight slowly melted into a wet grey morning, the travellers told themselves that they had made their ascent in vain. Suddenly one cried to the other, " Look up ! " High in heaven, above earth-born cloud and dimness, there towered a vision of shining Alpine summits—the bastions of

Italy—with the snowy peaks of Monte Rosa
aglow in the flush of the dawn.

To lift up our eyes on high is the medicine
for despondency, the antidote against dismay.
We walk about Zion, and lament over ecclesiastical dilapidations which we have no skill
to repair—as though the Heavenly Architect
Himself were not repeating His perpetual
promise : " I will build My Church." When
once by faith we look up above the kingdoms
and cathedrals of this world, we can rejoice in
the King Eternal, Immortal, Invisible, Who
is reigning in holiness and love. Even amid
the tumult of anarchy and revolution, our
hearts grow tranquil as we worship before His
great white throne. Then we know that the
judgments of the Lord are true and righteous
altogether. In quietness and confidence we
commit ourselves to the God Who has remembered us and redeemed us. By His grace He
renews our strength, so that through all the
shadowy months and years before us we shall
walk and not faint.

How many Christians suffer their hearts to
grow entangled and preoccupied with objects
not in themselves mean or unworthy, but
lower than the Supreme Object of all ! If our
prayers miscarry, it is often because we think
too much about the things which we desire and
the requests which we offer, and too little about
Him with Whom we have to do when we pray.
For in our petition we are not dealing with His

priests or with His courtiers : we are speaking
face to face with God Himself. So also, when
our expectations go bankrupt, it is often because
we do not cherish each purpose and pursue
each plan, as knowing that they are plans and
purposes which God controls and which God
in His mercy may frustrate. Those who lift
up their eyes steadfastly to heaven learn how
futile it is for a man to make certain of any
events on earth. The thread of our expectation
is thin, and easily snaps. But we are taught
by the Spirit to sit loose from all our expectations, and to see God's finger in their failure as
much as in their fulfilment. We come to
understand at last that God Himself—and no
lower good than Himself—is the fulfilment of
every hope, the satisfaction of every desire,
the answer to every prayer. And as we humbly
wait upon His will, we hear in the stillness a
Divine Voice whispering : "Behold, I am thy
Friend, and thy Shield, and thine exceeding
great Reward."

I AM THE WAY

AMONG the words of Christ which St. John's
Gospel has treasured up, none is more wonderful
than His sentence, " *I am the Way, the Truth,
and the Life.*" That short, simple, unsearchable saying carries us into the region of absolute

ideas. Its very terms—Life, Truth, Way—are
beyond our definition. Each of them opens
up deep vistas of meaning, full of thoughts
which do wander through eternity. Yet we
may recognize at least from these words that
Christianity involves a character and a creed
and an experience, and that all three are bound
up in our Lord's own Person. For He does
not merely tell us, " I reveal the way, I explain
the truth, I impart the life " : but He affirms
" I am all these things Myself." . . . " The
perfect ideal of goodness, it is I : follow Me.
The open secret of knowledge, it is I : learn of
Me. The eternal fountain of life, it is I : if
any man thirst, let him come unto Me and
drink."

When Christ says " I am the Way " we may
understand at least that Christianity means a
special kind of character. For in this world's
wilderness there are many ways, smooth and
stony, broad and narrow. Different races have
cherished their national ideals of manhood.
Different religions have formed their own types
and examples of virtue. Each great original
thinker has done something to individualize his
conception of what character ought to be; as
when Plato described the qualities of a true
citizen, or Comte elaborated the picture of a
servant of humanity. And not only philo-
sophers, but plain everyday people cannot help
being concerned about the conduct of their lives.
They are perplexed by the question, " What,

after all, is real goodness ? What is the right rule
to walk by ? What is the highest standard to
strive after and pursue ? " Now a Christian is
not left doubtful how to answer such questions.
Because Christ has already answered them,
once for all. Amid the movement of human
thought and the flux of human fashion, amid
the bewildering changes of what we are pleased
to call progress, there runs one supreme dominating Way. We see it marked out in history
through past generations. We can trace it
back to Him Who is its Author and Finisher,
Who says of Himself, " I am the Way."

The perfect ideal of character, the final
standard of conduct, is Christ Himself as He
shines on us in the pages of the New Testament.
We come face to face with Him in the Gospels,
and the Figure that meets us there is not vague
and shadowy, but clear and distinct and unlike
anyone else in the world. We recognize Him,
reflected and expressed more or less imperfectly
in His followers. The Christian type and
temper stand out distinct from all other types,
and persisting through long centuries of time.
The master-fact of the history of ethics is the
unmistakable moral likeness between those who
humbly confess that they are disciples and
imitators of Jesus Christ.

Among the evidences of our religion none is
more convincing than the miraculous manner
in which Christ has thus impressed the stamp
of His own lineaments upon men and women

naturally most unlike each other. He has brought together folk of diverse nations, cradled in alien ideas, and speaking strange tongues ; but more or less strongly they all remind us of Himself, they bear common witness to Him. Because wherever we see this character and way of life exemplified in the world we are driven to ask, " Is it from heaven or of men ? " And we are constrained to confess that it belongs to a Source and Origin which are divine.

The Godhead of Jesus is primarily manifested in His character. We worship Him not first of all for His mighty works, not even for His mighty words, but for His own sake, because He Himself compels our adoration. His gentleness and sternness, His compassion and courage, His burning tenderness and awful purity and measureless sacrifice—they blend into one arresting, conquering Personality, whereby we know Him to be God's Way in the world, the one Way in which we can travel to the sky.

Since Christianity involves a character, which is summed up in a Person, the aim and endeavour of Christians must be to reproduce that character by imitation of that Person. Our problems about the conduct of life all come back to Him for their solution. So much of the terror and pain of our existence here arises out of the strange waylessness of the world. We cannot trace any line of coherent purpose in our own lives or in the wider life of mankind. Often we feel like lost children who have missed the

track.   We can enter into the confession which
begins Dante's great poem :

> " In the mid-way of this our mortal life,
> I found me in a gloomy wood astray."

Baffled and perplexed, and worn out with
random wandering, we ask wistfully, " How
can we know the way ? "   Now in this sentence
the way to be trodden is lifted into a Personality
and identified with the Lord Himself.

It fortifies us to know that the path for us
to choose through time's maze and labyrinth
is not any matter of dubious speculation or of
abstruse definition.   It does not need to be
discovered and mapped out anew.   It is a road
already traced on earth by the print of Christ's
own footsteps ; and its milestones are His
beatitudes, and its guide-post is His Cross.
Pilgrimage grows simple as our thoughts turn
away even from our own stumbling feet, to fix
themselves on Him Who still says, " I am the
Way "—the same yesterday, and to-day, and
for ever.   Men are still asking the question,
" What is progress ? " and disputing wrathfully
or despairingly over their many answers.   But
Christians have solved the secret.   For each
true pilgrim of eternity, progress means going
forward, further and deeper, in Christ.   For it
is Christ Who makes Himself at once our Path
and our Companion, our Guide and our Goal.

IN His great saying, *I am the Way, the Truth, and the Life,* our Lord implies that Christianity involves not only a character, but a creed. He claims to be the one Way for us to walk in, and also the one Truth for us to know. When we consider the matter we may perceive that this follows, as a deeper aspect of Himself. For Christ could not be the Way unless He were the Truth as well. When He affirms, " I am the Way," fixed among the movement of human affairs and the flux of human opinions, that implies that He holds a corresponding place in the permanent order of existence. And when He declares, " I am the Truth," amid this world's shadows and illusions, He is claiming to embody in Himself the hidden Nature of things, to be one with the ultimate spiritual Reality. He tells us that to know Him is to enter into the secret of the heart of God.

We meet indeed not a few persons who accept Christ as the perfect Way, before they receive Him as the Eternal Truth. But the first logically involves the second. No sooner have we set foot in this Way, than we discover it to be no mere sentiment or dream but real and substantial and enduring, and so we are driven to meditate on that Truth, that basis in the nature of being, on which we are confident it must rest. Theology means an attempt to

12   177

think coherently about the facts of spiritual
existence and experience. And if we recognize
such facts at all, we cannot help trying to understand them rationally, and to express them
intelligibly. Too often men have made that
attempt proudly or perversely ; but make it
they must. For God, Who is the Eternal
Reason, has given us minds which compel us
to seek after the Truth and to believe that the
Truth must needs be consistent and coherent,
minds which will not let us believe that He
can leave us finally in intellectual confusion.
Every Christian has an implicit theology,
whether or no he confess it in formal words.
As a wise teacher has said : " A man's theology
is his theory of the universe. And our ideal
of life ought surely to rest upon a theory of
some kind. The man without a theology is in
danger of becoming a man without an ideal."
Sometimes, indeed, we hear people talk in
praise of undogmatic religion and a creedless
faith ; but such talk cannot be taken seriously.
It is only the impatient utterance of slip-shod
thinkers. For what is a doctrine ? It is
simply some spiritual fact expressed in intelli-
gent terms. What is a creed ? It is only
certain doctrines arranged in some rational,
orderly connexion. And what is a dogma ?
It is no more than some doctrine, which is
generally accepted and made the basis of united
action. Reasonable men cannot act together
in religion, or in politics, or in anything else,

without a ground of common conviction, and that conviction put into words is dogma. To borrow a familiar illustration, the statement with which the American Declaration of Independence opens and on which the constitution of the United States was founded—the statement that all men are by birth free and equal—is neither more nor less than a dogma. It is true enough that theology itself, like every other good thing, has too often been abused and perverted. We must be on guard continually against doctrines which are false, and creeds which pretend to be exhaustive, and dogmas which are wrongly applied. But we do not get rid of theology by rebelling against the name, and we cannot escape a creed by refusing to think it out or to write it down. Even the Lord's Prayer, simple as it sounds, takes an immense amount of theology for granted. And the *Te Deum* is itself a creed, framed as an anthem and set to music. Some one has said that if all the creeds which Councils ever framed were blotted out and forgotten, each cardinal doctrine of Christian faith might be recovered from the verses of the *Te Deum* alone.

The New Testament shows us plainly that Christianity involves a creed. Those who set themselves humbly and honestly to learn of Christ, as well as to follow Christ, are led into a common belief about Him. They discover that they are all in contact with one and the

same Reality. It is true, indeed, that we often
interpret our Lord as faultily as we imitate
Him. We misunderstand the Truth just as
we stumble in the Way. And so we ought to
deal with errors in doctrine not less tenderly
than we deal with frailties of conduct. The
perfect creed is as rare as the perfect character.
For an infallible theology we should need an
impeccable Church. Nevertheless Christ does
disclose to men definite facts about God and
the universe and human nature. And His
disciples learn to look at all things in a characteristic way. We learn to measure life and
death, and the issues of life and death, by the
measure of Christ Himself. We accept His
words when He tells us what we cannot verify
concerning the mysteries of the world to come.
And when any truth in this world appears to
our minds to be alien from Christ, we may
take this for a token that the time is ripe for
us to understand Christ better. Since no truth
can be alien from the Divine Reason, Whose
Word was made flesh.

For sincere and humble Christians, spiritual
growth means a progress from doubt and
dimness into clearer insight and deepening
certainty. Day by day they grow more at
home with Him Who is Himself the Truth of
all truths. The order of experience, as a gifted
theologian points out, corresponds with the
order of the Lord's promises, which He offered
to those who had begun to believe in Him : *If*

ye abide in My word, ye are truly disciples of Mine, and then *ye shall know the Truth, and* then *the Truth shall make you free.*

I AM THE LIFE

WHEN we meditate on our Lord's overwhelming saying, *I am the Way, the Truth, and the Life,* we approach the spiritual secret of the Gospel. For these profound words show us that Christianity involves not only a character, and a doctrine, but an experience as well ; and that all three are bound up in One Divine Person. Here is Christ's inmost thought concerning Himself : " I am the Life."

What is life ? Perhaps the best way in which we can define it is to say that life means the difference between a sleeper and a corpse. Yet the wisest of men have no skill to analyse that difference, or to explain wherein it consists. What does our Lord intend us to understand when He affirms, " I am the Life " ? To grasp the fullness of this sentence we must recollect that it fell from His lips the same night in which He was betrayed, when He had already entered the valley of the shadow of death. Once before He had spoken similar words, when He stood by the open grave of His friend —words which we never hear unmoved, by the open graves of our friends. " I am the Resurrection and the Life," said Christ—the Life,

and therefore the Resurrection, the vital essence
and energy which dying cannot destroy. And
once afterwards the same word came from a
Voice which was as the sound of many waters.
Out of the fullness of His kingdom and power
and glory, the Lord spoke to His servant John
saying, " I am the First, and the Last, and the
Living One." For that victorious Life, which
was laid down for men, is now reigning on the
throne of God.

Moreover, before we can feel how much is
involved in " I am the Life," we must understand that this saying sums up and harmonizes
and completes the thoughts of Christ as our
Truth, and Christ as our Way. When we have
tried to determine what goes to make up man's
personality, we discover that we cannot divide
human nature into compartments and shut it
off into exclusive sections. Character and
reason are indeed inseparable parts of the inner
self ; but they are not the whole of that to
which they belong. Life stands for our central
being and essence ; although it is Life indeed,
only as taught by the Truth and as exercised
in the Way. And so Christians receive Christ
not merely to rule their conduct and to mould
their thinking, but to dwell in the very citadel
and fortress of their souls. They find Him far
more than an ideal Example to imitate, far
more than a perfect Teacher to trust. They
find Him a vital inward Energy, to cleanse
and to inspire.

Herein lies the ultimate distinction between our Lord and all human prophets. Buddha could point his disciples to a way and say, " Walk ye in it." Socrates could tell his pupils of a truth and say, " Cleave ye to it." But He Who stands above all earthly guides and teachers, He Who though He was dead is alive again for evermore, is able to pour His own life into the spirits of foolish and selfish men until they are aware of a mighty Presence entering and possessing and transforming the depths of their being. Christianity is a divine experience—or it is nothing. We might almost say that a Christian is a person into whom Christ infuses part of His own Personality, so that new powers and motives and passions are stirred and quickened at the very springs of being. In the supernatural work of our salvation, " grace " really means that Christ, the Fountain of vital healing, is imparting Himself to sick and sinful souls. His regenerating Life comes to abide with them, to purify them from their corruption, to redeem them into new childhood, to kindle in them the flame of undying hope, to breathe into them the spirit of universal charity. Life is indeed much more than emotion, but emotion is its highest expression ; and Christ becomes our life as He sheds abroad in our hearts the Love of God— which is Himself.

Christianity involves a character, and a doctrine, and an experience. Well said Thomas

à Kempis : " Without a way, there is no going ;
without a truth, there is no knowing ; without
a life, there is no living." And the Way and
the Truth and the Life which are Christ's
cannot be found outside of Him. How amazing
is that exclusive claim : " No man cometh unto
the Father but by Me." Our Lord is warning
us not merely that He is the one Absolver and
Reconciler of the guilty, but that of Him, and
through Him, and by Him, are all things to the
believer. Apart from Him we can do nothing
that will seem worth doing, we can be nothing
that will seem worth being, judged in that
white light of reality which will so soon shine
upon us all. Christ Himself is our Way : to
make progress means to go on farther and
deeper into Christ. Christ Himself is our
Truth : to grow wise means to enter into the
secret of His wisdom and to keep on learning
more of Him day by day. And Christ Himself
is our Life, the Redeemer and Reviver and
Restorer of our spirits, the Author and Finisher
of our faith, the Pledge of our immortality.

THE FAITH OF THE SAINTS

In recent years men have turned, as they never
turned before, to the witness of Christian
experience. We are applying to theology the
method which has proved so fruitful in the
kingdom of science. We forsake the high *à*

priori road, and try to deduce our theories from carefully sifted facts. To quote the words of a living scholar : " In no branch of thought to-day can opinion rest on authority, apart from verifiable experience. Can it seriously be urged that the case of religion is exceptional ? " Now this method, when we apply it to the collective experience of the Church, leads at any rate to certain elementary conclusions. For instance, no observer will deny that Christian character has always existed as the outcome and product of Christian belief. History points to an unmistakable connexion between practical goodness and definite faith. You cannot build noble careers out of vague speculation and emotion ; you cannot get men to suffer and die for a peradventure. Confessors are made out of people who have something to tell, and martyrs out of people who have Someone to love. Whatever else may be true about the saints, one fact is quite obvious : they were saints because they possessed a real, positive faith. They knew Him Whom they trusted.

It is true enough that the saints are not perfect people. They have their defects and limitations. Some of them we might set down as prejudiced and superstitious and narrow-minded. In the New Testament " saint " does not generally imply a spotless character. It is used as the family name of the children of God. It means one who has the root of Christ's righteousness planted in his heart by faith.

The saints are the household of the faithful ; and their experience proves that, though Christianity is too profound and mysterious to be contained in any formula, it does involve a definite belief.

After so many generations the Gospel has not now for the first time to discover its own meaning. That meaning, indeed, has often been encrusted with errors and darkened with corruptions. But there never was an age since the Resurrection when Christians as a whole have been ignorant of the essence of their faith. The Church could not have kept alive if it had lost all loyalty to its Author and Founder. As we trace the golden thread of Christian experience running through the chequered centuries, we realize how the supernatural power and charm of holiness have always depended on a few great simple beliefs which the best Christians hold in common. Joubert has warned us that just as in poetry it is dangerous to disagree with the poets, so in religion it is dangerous to disagree with the saints. We may dispute and contend over theological and ecclesiastical differences until we forget that the substance of faith resides in those elemental truths concerning which the most Christ-like Christians agree.

If men inquire for a summary of belief which all Christians accept, they may discover it in the *Te Deum*—that ancient hymn, " We praise Thee, O God, we acknowledge Thee to be the Lord," which all Christians unite to sing. Of course, the *Te Deum* is not theology, it is adoration ; but for all that, it implies a positive and definite creed—the faith of the saints. It affirms those great revealing and redeeming acts of God which *are* the Gospel.

Again, when we ponder over this appeal to experience, we begin to understand why the faith of Christ has been committed to the saints to keep. It is not entrusted to theologians and religious thinkers as such ; too often they have perverted and obscured it. Nor is it delivered to priests and pastors and religious officials as such ; too often they have betrayed and lost it. The faith is delivered to the saints—that is, to the fellowship of faithful disciples, to plain men and humble women in whom Christ is reproducing something of His own likeness. The faith is safe in no other hands than theirs : for they have personal, immediate knowledge of what redemption means. But so long as the saints survive, so long as there are men and women in this workaday world who put us irresistibly in mind of the love of Christ, so long Christianity cannot die.

When we are exhorted to contend earnestly for the faith delivered to the saints, we must take heed that the stress falls not on the word " contend " but on the word " earnestly." We are faithful, not by being contentious, but by being earnest ; not by striving, or crying, or lifting up our voice in the streets, but by serious, ardent devotion to Him Whom having not seen we love. The Gospel is something to be in earnest about. Jesus Christ is the most transcendent of all facts, the most awful and glorious of all certainties. The spirit we have to dread is the spirit of dull, cynical indifference —the secret doubt whether anything really matters much : that is the temper which ruins the soul. But a true believer can never be too much in earnest. No Christian can ever love Christ too passionately, or serve Him too loyally, or sacrifice for Him too lavishly, or contend too ardently for the faith of the Crucified—which has been delivered to the saints.

O GOD, THOU ART MY GOD

THE Book of Psalms has been called the hymn-book of the Jewish Church, bequeathed as a legacy to all true children of faithful Abraham. We possess many precious volumes which have come down to us from early ages, but among them all not one is worthy to be compared with this. The heirlooms of ancient literature as a rule only interest scholars, while common people find them antique and musty and out-of-date. When they are translated, they sound like ghosts of the old world muttering in the language of the new. But the Psalter still speaks to men in their mother-tongue. Hoary with age, it is a book of to-day—a book which with all our modern progress we have not outgrown, which we never shall outgrow. Because these Psalms pierce down to the deepest needs and instincts of human nature. They deal with man's changeless hunger and hope and love and shame and anguish. They speak from the heart to the heart, concerning the heart's God. And so it comes to pass that whereas other ancient poems seem in comparison dull and scholastic, the Book of Psalms, like the Book of Nature, keeps all the freshness of immortal youth. It is no more stale and worn-out than the sunshine or the mountains or the sea.

No other book in the world is so sacred as this, or so dear to godly men and women. The Psalter is incorporated into the liturgy of every Church. It has become the text-book of Christian devotion. For each generation it has served as the grammar whereby men have learned how to think and to speak about their inward life. It has moulded and coloured the best men's best feelings, and given words to their most ardent prayers. Its voice has blended with the battle-cries and the cradle-songs of Christendom. What passionate confessions and petitions and thanksgivings have found utterance in its verses ! What multitudes of the dying have spent their last breath on its syllables—since the day when Jesus Christ

Himself died with a text out of the Psalms upon His lips.

Let us imagine that by some marvel such forgotten things could revive and come to light, and all these invisible and nameless associations could be made plain and marked down on the pages of the Psalter—what a book of wonders would be here ! Like some old manuscript, copied and crossed and recrossed with the traces of its history and its uses, so (says Dr. John Kerr) the Book of Psalms would show for what it really is—the great record and register of human experience, written over with the secret history of men's hearts, here blotted with the tears of repentance, here stained with the blood of martyrs, on every page illuminated with heavenly visions and made beautiful with the shining footprints of the messengers of peace. And when we seek refuge in Scripture from our own troubles, we turn from St. Paul's arguments, we turn even from our Lord's parables, and we go by instinct to the Psalms, these human utterances of men of like passions with ourselves—because they touch us and teach us and comfort us like no other portion of the Book of God.

When we take the Psalter and compare it with ordinary modern hymn-books, we become aware of one notable change. Quite beyond outward differences of structure and rhythm, there is what may be described as a difference of spiritual standpoint. The average modern hymn-writer is apt to think first and foremost about himself, his own inward condition and emotion. Whereas the Hebrew Psalmist looks away and forgets himself in adoration of the Most High. The Eternal God is his refuge, and the burden of his song. And he thinks of himself mainly as related to God. Thus, for instance, in Psalm xxxvii we read : " trust in the Lord," " delight thyself in the Lord," " commit thy way unto the Lord," " rest in the Lord "—each precept looking outward and upward. The only precept which looks inward warns us against so doing by a thrice-repeated injunction " fret not thyself." Why, the modern hymn-writer is fretting himself half his time. The tendency in question, however, is not confined to our hymn-books ; it infects our prayers and our sermons. There are some good men who practically preach faith, instead of preaching Christ. There are Christians who spend their time in questioning about faith and hope and love, instead of actually believing and hoping and loving. But a bird does not learn to fly by thinking about its wings. When I see clearly, I am not conscious of the eyeball or the retina. And when I believe properly, I am conscious only of Him Whom I have trusted : I cry " O God, Thou art my God."

Nor is it merely our own inward notions and feelings which we are tempted to put in the place of God Himself. Sometimes it is our theology or our ritual. " O creed, thou art my

creed, loudly will I recite thee "—" O Church,
thou art my Church, often will I visit thee "—
these are refrains which we are fond of chanting
to ourselves in a secret undertone.   Now things
like these—Church and creed and theology and
ritual—are sacred and necessary helps towards
the living God.   But when we treat them as
ends in themselves, instead of mere means,
they become our deadly hindrance.   The Psalm
which the redeemed can sing looks away from
all creatures to the Creator.   It forgets the
ladder of blessing in its vision of the All-
Blessed.   It cries out wistfully, passionately,
exultantly, " O God, Thou art my God. . . .
All my fresh springs are in Thee."

This experience which has God for its object
realizes God as its possession.   The Psalmist
dares to appropriate his Maker, he knows that
the Everlasting Love is his own.   He is not
afraid in utter humility to make the unspeakable claim : " O God, Thou art my God."
That sentence might be taken for the watchword, the formula of absolute religion.   It
begins in exile, it ends at home.   " O God,"
we cry, standing before the gateway of our
lost paradise, with dreadful faces thronged and
fiery arms—" O God, Thou art my God " : and
when we can say that, paradise is regained.
Happy are we, if we have learned to say it
with the same tender confidence, the same
sense of happy personal possession, with which
when we were little children we used to say

" my mother." Surely we have heard for ourselves, in quiet hours, on lonely nights, the Divine Voice whisper through the darkness : " O child, thou art My child. Early and late am I seeking thee."

THY WILL BE DONE

FEW men can seriously consider the universe, of which they themselves form a part, without coming to believe that it is one orderly coherent whole—a cosmos and not a chaos. It is impossible to think of nature as " an infinite litter of detail," produced by accident. Our common mistake to-day lies in the opposite direction. We are tempted to see nothing in the world but a unity of mechanical forces. " Law " is the spectre which haunts this generation. There are some Christians even who degrade the will of God by confusing it with sheer sovereignty. They say " Thy will be done," with the dreary fatalism of the Moslem who murmurs *kismet*, and accepts the inevitable which he has no power to avert. So you hear English people resign themselves (as they tell you) to Providence, with the air of making a pious virtue out of necessity : " When he would not be persuaded we ceased, saying : ' The will of the Lord be done.' " And if Almighty God were sheer Omnipotence and nothing more, men would cringe helplessly

13

before His might, and submit to the awful
Sultan in the sky.

Yet does not our deepest human instinct
revolt against such an attitude ? Even the
old pagan poets knew better. They pictured
Prometheus, chained to the rock, but hurling
defiance at the Power which tortured him,
because that Power was tyrannous and despotic
and vindictive. Whatever is noblest within
us refuses to grovel before blind brute Force,
however mighty. Conscience itself rises up in
wrath to demand that the Supreme shall be
supreme in goodness, if we are to yield ourselves
loyally to His sway. The Gospel teaches us
what God's will really means, by showing us
what God's nature really is. The order and
beauty of created things give us hints of a
Creator who is the source and secret of all order,
Himself the First and only Fair. But nature's
dumb witness is too feeble and conflicting to
prove what He proved, Who could say : " Lo !
I come, I delight to do Thy will, O my God."
For He Who thus delighted in the Father's will
and understood it utterly and fulfilled it
perfectly—He alone has manifested it completely. He has unveiled the Eternal Essence
from which that will proceeds. He has revealed
to a wondering world, which only half believes
the glorious, incredible truth, that the root of
God's will is goodness and the fountain of God's
heart is love.

Thy will be done. This shortest and simplest

clause in the Lord's Prayer is the hardest of all to pray. It sums up the last lesson of divine discipline rather than the first impulse of human nature. As soon as a child wakes up to know himself, we recognize that he has a will of his own. He begins to exercise that strange power of choice, without which we are not men at all. Yet even a child must submit to parents and teachers, and learn to do as he is bid. He must accept that authority which has a right to command. As we grow older and obtain the franchise of outward freedom, we feel on our spirits the stress of a mysterious claim within—the binding claim of duty. Christ's own voice repeats and ratifies the same solemn commandment. He speaks with the imperative of conscience itself when He forbids us to indulge our own self-will, and claims that we accept instead the holy will of God. Nay, He tells us that human nature takes its appointed place in the divine order as it obeys the divine precept, "Do as you are bid." This grandest and hardest of commandments is so hard because it challenges our pride ; and pride is the favourite sin of mankind. Who does not naturally enjoy having his own way ? Each of us has a will of his own ; but so long as it remains his own will it works his wretchedness and misery and ruin.

> " Our wills are ours, we know not how :
> Our wills are ours, to make them Thine."

To learn that lesson we often need a long lifetime of discipline. Only after shipwreck and defeat and desolation do we grow willing, " having tried all other ways, just to try God's." We have not faith enough to understand that our Father's will is nothing but pure and perfect love, and that the doing of it makes heaven to be heaven indeed.

The beatitude of Paradise is far grander than our poor dreams. It does not consist in the addition of all things pleasant and the subtraction of all things painful. It is that condition where God's will rules naturally, without discord and disobedience. Heaven means the state where everyone delights in pleasing God : and must it not follow that hell means the state of sheer wilfulness, where everyone does as he pleases ? The stars in their shining march are a pattern of the perfect order. The angels, who keep their first estate, live and move and have their rapture in the will of God. The song of the heavenly host is a parable of obedience : for there can be no harmony except as each singer and player follows the gesture of the Master of music. The spirits of the redeemed are made perfect in that celestial anthem, because on earth they began to learn its secret : *Not my will, but Thine be done.* To understand heaven, we must consider Him who came from the Father's bosom, to declare His will and to finish His work—the will that none should perish, the work of bearing away the sin of the

world. Christ is the revelation of heaven.
Even on earth, He had heaven always in His
spirit, because He was at one with His Father.
His heart is the heart of God, and His Passion
is the utterance of God's will towards men.
So we learn our obedience by the things which
He suffered. In our worst bereavement, our
sharpest anguish, our bitterest betrayal, we
frame our lips to whisper after Him : *Father, if
it be possible, let this cup pass . . . nevertheless,
not as I will, but as Thou wilt.*

Nevertheless this prayer, as Christ taught it
to His disciples, is not merely a private petition.
It embraces nothing less than the whole world.
When we say, " Thy will be done on earth, as
it is in heaven," we are praying against all
tyranny and cruelty and slavery, against all
oppression and corruption—wherever they exist
among men. We are praying for the victory of
redemption, for the conquest of the Gospel.
Nay, we are praying that heaven may come down
and renew the earth, and change winter into
spring.

Thy will be done : it is the prayer of jubilant,
triumphant faith. Too often we chant it
mournfully, like a dirge over dead hopes, a
lamentation for what God has taken away. We
are slow of heart to believe that the will of the
Father is bearing all souls that yield to it into
the joy of their Lord. The man who realizes
this, ceases to struggle with God's will, or
provide against it : he is " borne on unresistingly

into that blessedness to which it perpetually
presses to carry him.''

THEY SAW GOD AND
DID EAT AND DRINK

IT is easy to eat and drink without seeing God.
When we sit down to table, how many of us
realize with simple thankfulness that our meal
comes from the hands of our Father ? Yet
each common loaf bears witness that all over
the world for uncounted generations men have
gone on ploughing and sowing and reaping, that
they may win their bread out of the dust.
The rippling plains of wheat in Manitoba and
the Argentine still testify to the urgency of
human hunger—just as did the Syrian cornfield
through which Christ walked with His disciples
when they plucked the ripe ears on a Sabbath
day. How seldom we recollect that our race
has never one full year's supply of food in the
storehouse ! Mankind would starve and perish
within twelve months if it were not for God's
recurring bounty in the harvest. Concerning
earth's hungry multitudes we may say : '' The
eyes of all wait upon Thee, and Thou givest
them their meat in due season. Thou openest
Thine hand, and satisfiest the desire of every
living thing.''

Again, men are surely blind to God when
they eat and drink to excess. And in spite of
civilization many persons have failed to learn

the elements of self-restraint. Though they were made a little lower than the angels, they often make themselves only a little higher than the brutes. It is true that during the last half-century Englishmen have left off admiring drunkenness. Intoxication no longer seems manly, it hardly seems amusing. We confess it to be a degradation of human nature ; yet it remains one of our chief national vices. Luxury, moreover, has many sides. The chief baker can minister to self-indulgence as really as the chief butler. It may be said that animal sensualism is condemned by good taste and good breeding. Belshazzar's feast was not merely godless, it was vulgar as well. Yet there are crowds of people who in the general conduct of their lives behave as if God were absent or extinct. Men who are temperate and clever and refined steadily shut their eyes to things eternal. Students explore the order of nature and unravel the courses of history, but they discern no Will that moulds it, no Heart that beats through it all. Artists interpret the glory of the world's loveliness, with no vision of Him who is the First and Only Fair. And in daily life we meet multitudes of secular persons who go on week after week doing their work, laying their plans, making their money, enjoying their pastimes, without any serious thought of their Maker, their Lover, their Judge ; without any concern for that strict and solemn account which they must render Him at last.

Again, there are some men who see God, but can neither eat nor drink. It is no uncommon experience that high exaltation of spirit will overpower the present sense of bodily needs. Our Lord Himself in the stress of temptation went fasting forty days in the wilderness. St. Paul, after his blinding vision, was three days and did neither eat nor drink. And we still find that the shock of calamity or the agony of bereavement can deaden physical appetites. The eternal realities come so close that we are dazed, like men that dream. But besides those whose overwhelming sense of the Divine unfits them for the world, there are others who err in their interpretation of the Divine and so shut themselves away from the world. Few half-truths have exerted such influence on Christendom as the ascetic ideal. Monks and hermits argued that because business and happiness often distract men from God, therefore to be perfect we must renounce natural pleasures and take refuge in the cave or the cloister from human society. So these ardent souls fled into poverty and solitude, and embraced hard discipline and meagre diet and coarse raiment and weary vigils—as steps on the ladder to heaven.

Nevertheless, true saintliness does not trample upon that human nature which God has created. Our natural instincts and appetites can be abused into instruments of self-indulgence and self-destruction ; but in themselves they are

good and not evil, they are meant to become
vehicles of blessing, helps to the holy life. The
complete Christian is neither an ascetic nor a
recluse. His pattern is not the lonely, austere
prophet, of whom it is written, " John came
neither eating nor drinking." His exemplar
is the Son of Man, who counted nothing human
to be alien from Himself. Forasmuch as the
children are partakers of flesh and blood, He
also Himself likewise took part of the same.
He lived in a cottage and plied a workman's
trade. He leaned on earthly friendship, and
gathered the little ones in His arms, and mixed
with common men and women—nay, they cast
it in His teeth that He ate and drank with
publicans and sinners. Jesus Christ could do
that, because in the soul of each publican and
each sinner He saw God.

Here is our Christian privilege and our
Christian duty. We have to use the world, as
not abusing it. We are not to despise it as
though we were too high and good for human
nature's daily food. We have to hold the
balance true between the flesh and the spirit ;
not to become absorbed in time so as to forget
eternity ; not to grow dazzled in dreams of
eternity so as to be heedless of daily duties and
indifferent to simple pleasures and blind to the
brightness and delight which God grants us
even in this low mortal world.

Our Lord Himself commanded His disciples
to commemorate His death by eating bread and

drinking wine. In that communion of the gathered Church it is the experience of Christians that they realize His presence in the midst of them. They confess that in that service they see God as they eat and drink. And yet the full sacramental truth is even more profound and wonderful. We have not to limit spiritual virtue to certain acts, however sacred ; we have to see the whole world and human life and duty transfigured into one great sacrament, wherein God enshrines His glory, whereby He imparts His grace. To faithful and surrendered souls their common fellowship becomes sacramental ; they learn to eat and drink their daily meals worthily, humbly, thankfully, eucharistically, discerning the Lord's body in them all.

THE HEART AND THE TREASURE

It has been said that no apostle, no New Testament writer, remembers Jesus Christ. For we can only remember those whom we have known in the past ; and they never think about Him as belonging to the past. For them, the Lord Who has lived and taught and suffered and died on earth is still perpetually present in the power of His risen life, exalted above the limits of time and space and reigning over the universe of God. So these early Christians seek the things that are above by a kind of natural instinct, because Christ is there, seated at God's right hand. And Christ Himself has told them : *Where your treasure is, there will your heart be also.*

The Gospel of the grace of God refuses to let us linger even amid the sacred scenes of the Nativity, the Ministry, the Passion. It constrains us to fasten our faith on Him Who is to-day the Resurrection and the Life of the world. Half the failures and perversions of Christianity have originated in forgetfulness of this cardinal truth. To take one example only : who can measure the incalculable harm which has been wrought by the adoration of the crucifix ? That mischief arises not so much because a crucifix is a graven image—for it may be argued that nearly all sacred art violates the letter of the second Commandment, according to its Jewish interpretation. The chief evil of crucifix-worship has been that it has distorted the Gospel by fixing men's thoughts exclusively upon Christ dead, rather than upon Christ risen and reigning. Whereas by the writers of the New Testament even " Christ Who is our Sacrifice " is transfigured and translated into " Christ Who is our Life." The earliest Christians worshipped their Redeemer not so much as the Victim expiring in mortal agony, but as the King of Love reigning in immortal light. And the introduction of the crucifix in lieu of the vacant cross was a token of the gradual saddening and weakening of the soul of Christendom which went on during the middle ages.

In more than one passage St. Paul points to
the primitive ritual of baptism as a symbol
which sets forth how the believer is identified in
spirit with Christ's death and with Christ's
resurrection. When our hearts are drawn into
mystical union with Him Who is our Treasure,
we also are conformed to His dying. Our
pride is nailed to His cross, our selfishness is
slain and buried in His sepulchre, our love rises
with Him into newness of heavenly life—a life
which is hid with Christ in God. St. Paul
conceives of the Christian as one who has passed
through this inward experience of dying, and
has been lifted into the eternal order where
Christ is alive for evermore. And therefore
the Christian's whole point of view is altered,
and his standards of judgment are changed, so
that for him ascetic rules and legal observances
no longer possess any inherent virtue of their
own.

It is difficult for us to bring home to ourselves
the full force of the apostle's argument, " If
ye died with Christ from the elements of the
world, why do ye subject yourselves to ordi-
nances after the precepts and doctrines of
men ? " For how can we enter into the state
of mind of a man who has solved the great
secret and endured that unutterable experience
which we call dying ? In one of John Foster's
letters he tries to imagine what it will be like
hereafter to look back upon death as something
actually accomplished, which lies behind you,

an event concerning which you can say, " It
is finished." In Browning's wonderful *Epistle
of Karshish, the Arab Physician,* the poet has
pictured how Lazarus lived after he came back
from his sojourn in the unseen world, how such
a one was continually aware of invisible realities,
how henceforth he could not help measuring
earthly things by heavenly standards of value.

> " The spiritual life around the earthly life :
> The law of that is known to him as this,
> His heart and brain move there, his feet stay here."

Is not that a parable of the fashion in which
they who are translated with Christ into the
eternal order must needs contemplate human
affairs, as from a divine vantage ground ?
After all, how many things are there on earth
which really matter, when they are viewed with
Christ's eyes, from the right hand of God ?

The answer must be, that nothing seriously
matters, except the inward possessions of a
heart united to Christ. As we realize and
possess Him who is our Treasure, we learn to
think as He thinks concerning things like
money and comfort and reputation and success.
While we come to understand also why the
New Testament lays such enormous emphasis
on the things of the spirit—on compassion, and
humility, and meekness, and pureness ; on
longsuffering, and forbearance, and forgiveness ;
and on love, which is the bond of perfectness ;
and on the peace which passeth all understanding ; and on thankfulness and praise.

For let us recollect, finally, that the experience of one who has his heart dwelling with Christ will be rich with jubilant music. The life which our Lord communicates is His own exalted life : and that is in its essence " love, joy, empire, victory." To quote the words of a great living theologian : " Christianity has been named the Religion of Sorrow ; but there never was a more complete misnomer. It is not the religion of sorrow, but the religion which, because it is inspired by One Who lives and *was* dead, gives the victory over every sorrow, even the crowning sorrows of death and sin. There is not in the New Testament from beginning to end, in the record of the original and genuine Christian life, a single word of despondency or gloom. It is the most buoyant, exhilarating, and joyful book in the world."

THEIR VOICE CANNOT BE HEARD

THE opening verses of the nineteenth Psalm, *Coeli enarrant*, find their best commentary in Coleridge's " Hymn before Sunrise in the Valley of Chamounix." No mere explanation in prose can interpret such high spiritual rapture. The Hebrew Psalmist knew little enough about the sun and the stars of which he sang. He was ignorant in regard to their masses and their motions. But because he was a prophet and a poet, he discerned in them the revelation of God.

To him, this brave, o'erhanging firmament was a scroll written over with its Creator's beauty. To him, this majestical roof, fretted with golden fire, was the vaulting of the temple of the Most High—a temple full of worship, where light and darkness are telling of God's glory, and life and death are singing in God's praise. To secular persons that temple may seem empty and desolate, for its praise is not framed by mortal lips nor its anthem set to earthly music. As we read in the Revised Version of the English Bible : *There is no speech nor language ; their voice cannot be heard.* But to the Psalmist, nature's great silence becomes expressive, and underneath the hush of the dumb creation he is aware of harmonious voices speaking unutterable words.

Alone on the hills at night, even the most prosaic man will confess that there is something sublime in that profound and perpetual stillness, which puts our human restlessness to shame. We can only work amid hurry and confusion and clamour. But God's eternal energies act so quietly, that for the most part we forget them. The clouds float and the seeds grow and the trees bud without a sound.

> " Each nightly star in silence burns,
> And every day in silence turns
>   The axle of the earth.
> The silent frost with mighty hand
> Fetters the rivers and the land
>   With universal chain ;

And, smitten by the silent sun,
The chain is loos'd, the rivers run,
The lands are free again."

And behold, summer has spread out her green banners noiselessly, before ever we are aware.

Consider some of those things which we neglect because they are so quiet, and ignore because they are as inaudible as dreams. They have no speech nor language ; their voice cannot be heard. First, God's judgments are silent. At times, indeed, a sudden calamity challenges all men's attention. Some popular idol lies shattered across his own threshold, some great fraud recoils upon its promoters, some rotten empire crashes down into the dust. But for the most part God's judgments are not noisy or sensational. The old Greek poet pictured with what stealthy steps the Furies follow a guilty soul ; and because he hears no tramp of doom behind him, no voice of doom above, he fancies that vengeance has missed his track. In this world retribution generally is a silent work. Day by day, and hour by hour, God is judging our sin. That selfish man, who seems so prosperous—his heart is shrivelling within his own breast. That lover of money—his inward nature is becoming cankered. That proud man, who will not forgive, is himself hardening beyond hope of repentance. That profligate has evaded public condemnation, but the black stain is sinking into his soul. Quietly the awful doom moves on, though there be no speech nor language and its voice cannot be heard.

Again, God's mercies are silent. Sometimes, indeed, He grants us an unexpected bounty, or works for us a signal deliverance ; but His best blessings after all are His commonest and His quietest. When God doeth alms, it is not with the sound of a trumpet. So we take His gifts as matters of course ; we hardly notice them until, perhaps, we wake up startled to find that they are gone. How many of us thank God for our health, while we enjoy it ; or for our reason ; or for our education ; or again for our national liberty ; or for the treasures of learning and delight which are garnered for us in books ? And how many of us are grateful as we ought to be for the blessing of friendship ? Now and again a man opens his eyes and is astonished at the quiet, patient affection he has been receiving, and marvels that his friend, who is so much nobler and wiser than himself, should care for him with such devotion. Best among earthly blessings is loyal, generous, human love —for it comes nearest to the Divine Love, which is utterly generous and eternally faithful. Yet this heavenly affection also is sometimes silent. When we walk amid shadows, our Unseen Friend may seem a great way off ; there is no speech nor language. But the tender mercy of the Lord is not less tender because there are times when His voice cannot be heard.

14

For God's messages also are silent. In most cases they do not come to us audibly—not in syllables of thunder or by the sound of an angel's tongue—not always from the lips of a preacher, or even by the sentences of Holy Writ. God speaks by a still small Voice, which uses no human words at all. When we have been able most vividly to realize the Invisible, it was not through any experience of speech or language. When God's mystic messengers draw near the soul,

> " They stroke us with a subtle grace.
>   We say, Who passes ?   They are dumb :
>   We cannot see them go or come ;
> Their touches fall like flakes of snow
>   Upon a blind man's face."

And if God's deepest messages are often inarticulate, so in like manner are men's holiest prayers. Two earthly friends can communicate without speech or language, by a look, a sign, a gesture ; and how much closer is the inward communion between the creature and the Creator ? We are careful and troubled over-much about the phraseology of devotion. We have lived too long upon the alms-basket of words. A Christian's most effectual and fervent prayer does not depend upon grammar. It is the soul's sincere desire, uttered or unexpressed. It is the burden of a sigh, the falling of a tear, the upward glancing of an eye when none but God is near. We pray most acceptably when we pray to our Father in secret, even in silence, when our voice cannot be heard. Worship did not cease when once, it is written, there was silence in heaven.

Therefore may God in His mercy preserve us from putting our trust in any words, or phrases, or formulas. May He lead us beyond these shadows to the eternal Substance. May He bring us to grasp the Divine realities which break through human language. May He keep us secretly in His pavilion from the strife of tongues.

THE CLOUD AND THE SEA

WHEN St. Paul wrote to the Corinthians : *I would not, brethren, have you ignorant, how that our fathers were all under the cloud, and all passed through the sea,* he was reminding his friends that God's ancient people had shared one common lot. In their tribulations and in their deliverances, they had all fared alike. When Israel came out of Egypt, the same watery gulf opened to give them passage, and baptized them together in its spray. The same mystic cloud guided their march across the desert, and brooded in gloom and glory over their pilgrim camp. In the experience of the ancestors of the Hebrews there had been no difference : " now these things happened unto them by way of example ; and they were written for our admonition, upon whom the ends of the ages are come." They stand for our admonition still. They warn us against two opposite errors, lest on the one hand we disdain the past, and on the other hand we idealize the past.

Many persons to-day, in the Church as well as in the world, look down with a certain contempt upon every century before the twentieth century. They are intoxicated with pride in modern inventions and discoveries. They gaze back scornfully at the benighted generations when newspapers and telephones and airships were unknown. Nevertheless, with all our new knowledge, man's inmost needs and sorrows and yearnings are not changed a whit. Mr. Frederic Harrison could not be called an obscurantist, and he has left this testimony : " Every aspect and appliance of practical life has been transformed within my own memory— and yet in all its essential conditions human life remains the same." We are strangers and sojourners as our fathers were. The same temptations torment us, the same mysteries baffle us, the same sorrows pierce us, the same grave waits for us in a little space.

Again, there is a converse error which is perhaps even more common among Christian people : we idealize the past. To our eyes bygone ages appear glorified in a mist of sacred memory. We imagine that holy men of old must have been quite unlike their degenerate descendants. And we excuse ourselves, by assuming that the saints and heroes and martyrs enjoyed some rare privileges and immunities which are denied to us now. Surely they must have been exempt from our humdrum trials, our prosaic duties. We cannot believe that they were in all points tempted, and succoured, like as we are. Nevertheless it remains true that the Christian's spiritual environment, his moral helps and hindrances, were substantially the same in earlier ages as they are now. Although so much has changed outwardly, yet the deep elemental things, the things that seriously matter, abide and endure. Human life varies but little in its main issues. Birth and marriage and death still go on in the ancient fashion. Seed-time and harvest, hunger and labour, love and pain and parting, are still the great controlling factors in man's lot. These things we have always with us. We also are all under the cloud, we all pass through the sea.

Men often feel that life grows more complicated and bewildering than it was once. The world we have to live in seems so confused, the path of duty so perplexing, the meaning of existence so obscure. Yet assuredly this is no new thing. The problems which we cannot solve haunted Plato and St. Paul. The deep questions which torment poor men and women lying on their sick-beds to-day are the very questions debated in the Book of Job by dark-eyed shepherd chieftains under the curtains of their tents in the morning of the world. Why do we have to suffer, and to suffer so unequally ?

What is the use of pain and loss and tragic
bereavement ? What does God mean by all this
mysterious trouble of human life ? What will
be the issue of it at last ? Our fathers were all
under the same cloud. They were torn with
doubts and fears, just as we are. Even in the
ages of faith, men walked by faith, not by sight
—just as we have to walk still. Their psalm
was only an earlier version of ours : " Lead,
kindly Light, amid the encircling gloom."
And they could only cling, just as we cling, to
the one unseen, unfailing Guide of them that
travel to the sky.

And our fathers all passed through the sea—
the sea of sorrow as well as the cloud of doubt.
A great sufferer has testified " man that is born
of a woman hath but a short time to live and
is full of misery." Who among us that is old
enough to be acquainted with grief will refuse
to endorse that ancient testimony ? Our
mothers baptized us with their tears, just as
we in turn baptize our own children. For us,
as for primitive folk, work is wearisome, and
disappointment is bitter, and war is dreadful,
and parting is sharp, and loss is cureless and
beyond repair. To-day, as in old time, we must
pray *De profundis clamavi*, " Out of the depths
have I cried unto Thee, O God. . . . The waters
are gone over my soul." Our fathers all passed
through the same sea. *Beloved, think it not
strange concerning the fiery trial which is to try
you, as though some strange thing had happened.*

God is dealing with us as He dealt with our fathers. He is leading us by the same steep and thorny road which all His saints had grace to tread.

Let us not be ignorant, therefore, of this catholic experience which dwells deep in the general heart of true believers. Sometimes we are tempted to gaze enviously at persons who seem high above us in their spiritual gifts and privileges—tempted to say, " Ah ! if I had that man's powers and opportunities and endowments, I might be as good a Christian and accomplish as noble a work." But they are all under the cloud, they all pass through the sea. The dauntless champions of faith have to conquer legions of cowardly doubts in their own souls. The bravest workers in God's Church have to wrestle against secret depression and lassitude and despair. There is no difference. The same Lord over all is rich unto all that call upon Him. As He dealt with our fathers, so will He deal with us. The clouds we so much dread are big with mercy and bright with lovingkindness, and through the very heart of the sea God still makes a way for His ransomed ones to pass over. Until He brings us at last to join our fathers and mothers and all the companies of the faithful, in that land where there shall be no more cloud and no more sea ; where love is an unerring light, and joy its own security.

SCRIPTURE is full of fighting. The Old Testament has been called the Book of the wars of the Lord. The Psalms of David were written by a soldier. And at the end of the New Testament a vision meets us of the armies that are in heaven, and of One, arrayed in a garment and vesture dipped in blood, who rides as Captain of the knights of God. Nevertheless, while on its surface the Bible reads like a book of battle, when we search more deeply we discover that it is the book of peace. Beyond time's crying and tumult the passion of the eternal conflict between good and evil resolves itself at last into passionless calm. Those that are redeemed from the earth stand upon a sea of glass, whose waves have been hushed into tranquillity. They have gotten the victory over all storms and sorrows, and they enter into everlasting rest.

Now we miss our way in the Bible unless it is leading us also to enter into rest—a rest which grows more profound and impregnable as years go by. The surest token of a Christian is that he has found peace with God. And though he may suffer the loss of all things beside, he need never forfeit his share in the peace which is Christ's parting legacy to His friends. When our Lord said, "Peace I leave with you, My peace I give unto you," He was

thinking of the supreme quality of that peace
wherewith His own soul was quiet—the living
peace which comes from being one with the
Father and delighting in the Father's will.
He meant that the peace of the very Heart of
the Universe was henceforth open for men to
enter : the peace of God Himself which passeth
all understanding—which the world cannot
give, and all the wars in the world cannot take
away.

This deep spiritual possession is a treasure of
which outward calamities and disasters have
no power to rob us. Nevertheless we ourselves
may spoil it and destroy it. So the emphasis
of the Psalmist's admonition falls on the third
word : " Fret not *thyself.*" How wonderfully
such a warning fits in with the facts of human
experience ! It lays its finger on the secret of
our obscure inward trouble—the self-imposed
burden, the self-inflicted torment, the self-
created pain. Psalm xxxvii points to various
ways in which Christian people so often vex
themselves and ruin their own peace.

For example, there is the way of envy.
Many a heart is consumed with hidden jealousies.
The Psalmist confesses that he fell into this
temptation when he saw the prosperity of the
wicked. Nothing vexes a man so sorely as his
bitter sense of unfairness in the ordering of
things. Then there is the way of repining. We
grieve over those good gifts which God has taken
away. We indulge in the luxury of grief over

their departure. We go to weep at the graves of dead hopes and buried failures.

Again, there is the way of foreboding. In these dark days multitudes are filled with anxiety about the morrow. They dread to think of what may be waiting for them a few weeks or months ahead. Yet how earnestly Christ rebuked this sin of foreboding. What royal, serene confidence sounds in His voice : " When ye hear of wars and rumours of wars, see that ye be not troubled." " Fear not " is God's command to His best and strongest servants. When an angel appears in the Bible he commonly begins his message by saying, " Fear not " ; in fact, you can often tell who he is by this angelic habit of salutation.

Then again, men fret themselves by impatience. They are hungry for recognition and appreciation. They get so weary of waiting for it. They ask, " Will my chance ever arrive ? Will my turn ever come ? " And, worst of all, we fret ourselves with self-pity. Nothing does more to spoil a man's inward peace than this impure spirit. He condoles with himself, and commiserates himself. He is touched with the pathos of his own condition, and cries, "Was ever grief like mine ! " All these evil things— envy and repining and foreboding and impatience and self-pity—increase as we indulge them ; they grow worse as they are fostered and cherished ; they make the heart raw. " Fret not thyself : *it only tendeth to evil.*"

The psalm is partly negative and partly positive. It warns us what to avoid. Cease from anger and forsake wrath. Refuse to harbour jealousy. Set your mind resolutely against repining and foreboding. Refuse to count the rankling wounds of self-love. Be ashamed of pitying your own condition. A wise stoic could say as much as that. But turn to the positive precepts : trust in the Lord, wait on the Lord, rest in the Lord, delight thyself in the Lord. The secret of peace is to turn away from our troubles to Him Who is the Rest, the Reward, the Delight of His children. Turn from evil-doers to Him Who does all things well. Turn from the prosperity of the proud to Him Who was despised and rejected of men. Turn from the workers of iniquity to the perfect work of Him Who can say already, " It is finished."

For Jesus Christ kept all the commandments of God, and realized all the beatitudes. When evil-doers compassed Him about, when the powers of hell gat hold upon Him, His heart was not troubled, neither was it afraid. He went out to meet death, and what was unfathomably more awful than death, with the quietness of assured victory. Already, He said, *the prince of this world is judged*. Even while the hosts of wickedness gathered to overwhelm Him, He saw the sentence of doom and destruction written upon them all. What else is there in history, or fiction, comparable to the

Son of God, on that same night in which He
was betrayed, gazing clear-eyed through agony
and desertion, discerning the cross and the
shame and the darkness, beholding Himself
laid in the sepulchre with a great stone rolled
upon His grave. He saw all that, to come before
another sunset ; and as He looked round on
His timid, tearful disciples, baffled in their fond
hopes of the coming kingdom, He could say,
" Be of good cheer ; I have overcome the
world."

No forger ever invented that kingly faith and
courage. It is too God-like not to be true.
The glory of Christ's conquering countenance
falls upon our fretfulness and foreboding, our
self-pity and repining, and they shrivel up and
sink out of sight. We forget our rivals, we
forget our injuries, we forget our anxious fears,
we forget even ourselves—we are caught up
into the rapture and the victory and the joy
of our Lord.

THE DIMENSIONS OF THE CROSS

At a season of bloodshed and anguish, when
there is darkness over all the earth, Passion
week comes home to us with power and meaning
which it never had before. As we sit over-
whelmed and confounded by tidings of human
suffering and misery and slaughter on a scale
too vast for the mind to take in, we are drawn

by irresistible attraction to contemplate the
redeeming agony of God. Here, at least, is no
shallow optimism, no evasion of the heart-
shattering facts. When we turn to gaze upon
the eyes and brow of Him Who was indeed
acquainted with grief, we are met there by " a
look of solemn recognition, such as might pass
between friends who had endured together some
strange and secret sorrow, and were united by
it in a bond which cannot be broken." When
we bow our knees before the Cross we are
pierced with the sense of its awful reality, we
begin dimly to apprehend with all saints what
is the breadth and length and height and depth—
and to know the Love which passeth knowledge.

Among the early Fathers some interpreted
those words, half fancifully, half mystically, as
pointing to the actual dimensions of the Cross
itself. And there is a sense in which it may be
said that the true Cross is as wide as humanity ;
it is as long as time ; it is as high as heaven ;
it is as deep as hell. To measure that Cross,
in its spiritual breadth and length and height
and depth, is to be filled with the fullness of
God. The words of the ancient psalm come
true when we apply them to the Crucified and
say : " If I ascend up into heaven, Thou art
there ; if I make my bed in hell, behold, Thou
art there. If I take the wings of the morning
and dwell in the uttermost parts of the sea,
even there shall Thy pierced hand hold me."
The Divine Passion is narrowed by no limits of

time or place. " Slain before the foundation of the world " is the testimony of the Apocalypse. " For the sins of the whole world " writes the apostle. In his wonderful prayer for the Ephesians, St. Paul implies that the dimensions of the true Cross are a sacred mystery. That Cross spreads its arms beyond the range of what our thoughts can think or our hearts conceive. We shall never explore it and exhaust it, until we borrow the golden reed of the angel to measure its breadth and length and height and depth—until we enter into God's incommunicable secret, which He hath reserved for them that love Him.

Yet there is a school wherein even simple Christians can be initiated into this mystery. We may read something of its purpose, we may grasp part of its meaning—enough to live by and to die by—in one way. St. Paul tells us what that way is : " ye may apprehend, with all the saints." The Gospel has not been all these centuries on earth for nothing. People to-day are not just beginning to find out who Christ is, and to discover for the first time what His Cross means. The Church has survived by holding fast to the elemental simplicities of the faith once for all delivered to the saints. The best Christians in every generation, the faithful folk of all countries and all communions, the poor in spirit and the pure in heart, have not gone altogether astray concerning the mystery of the Cross. We too may apprehend its meaning, as in our experience we keep company with them.

In the catholic experience of all saints we discover at least three cardinal elements—the sense of guilt, and of sorrow, and of sacrifice. Each element forces itself upon us vividly, against the lurid background of war. We know that we are living in a guilty world. Even if we believe that we belong to a nation which is fighting with clean hands and stainless conscience, we know that nothing but black, unutterable wickedness has brought this horror upon mankind. Face to face with the mystery of iniquity, the Cross reveals the mightier mystery of God's atonement and reparation and retrieval. As we remember millions of men, maimed and wounded, smitten and dying, we hear a Voice saying : " He was wounded for our transgressions, He was bruised for our iniquities : the chastisement of our peace was upon Him ; and with His stripes we are healed."

So again we realize now, more than ever before, the anguish and desolation of bereavement. Why are tears so salt ? Why are partings so bitter ? Why is loss so cruel ? To the most sorrowful enigmas of experience God gives us no explicit answer. But, forasmuch as the children are partakers of flesh and blood, He likewise Himself took part in the same. In His wounds all our human sorrows hide themselves, and our human self-denials support themselves against His Cross.

And we are living, not only in a world of mourners, but in a world of heroic sacrifice. Multitudes of men pass by to-day, singing as they march to face death for the sake of others. As we listen, deep down at the roots of our being we become aware of the kingdom and the power and the glory of sacrifice. The Cross reveals that spiritual mystery in all its breadth and length and height and depth. For the Cross is the sacrament and symbol of Love's infinite Passion—which lives eternally in the heart of God.

AT THE RIGHT HAND OF GOD

WHEN we think and speak about the things which are unseen and eternal, we can only use ideas and language which are borrowed from things seen and temporal. We speak, for example, about the Ascension of Christ, and we read in the Gospel that "He was taken up into heaven,"—as though God and heaven were actually any more above us than beneath us or within us. We employ the images of time and space and carry them into that spiritual realm where they have no proper meaning. Yet this is our infirmity, when we remember the years of the right hand of the Most High. We confess that our Lord ascended into heaven—although He had heaven round about Him always, and He brought heaven with Him into the midst of His disciples as often as He showed Himself alive to them after His Passion by many infallible proofs. Nevertheless, it was expedient for them that He should go away, that He might become no longer a local but a universal Presence. For the Ascension does not mean mere change of locality. It means a passing to God, concerning Whom we cannot say that He is in this place rather than in that. Christ Himself abides unchanged in personal character, now that He has passed into the absolute and perfect order of being. He has carried our human nature with Him into the bosom of the Father from whence He came, and into the glory which was His own before the foundation of the world. Having ascended into heaven, He sitteth at the right hand of God.

This last figure of speech, as Westcott pointed out, suggests two main ideas. It speaks of a work accomplished. Among men, he who sits down has completed his task and enters into rest. So our Lord, when He was dying, could say concerning the redemption which He wrought : " It is finished." The endless sacrifice has been offered once for all. He Who endured its cross and despised its shame hath sat down at the right hand of the throne of God. But further, this figure of speech suggests not only a work accomplished, but also a kingdom won. It implies sovereignty, as well as repose. The Son of God reigns supreme in the eternal world. Love all-suffering has proved itself also almighty.

15

The King of kings has led captivity captive, and He must reign till He has put all enemies under His feet.

Ascension Day calls us upward and onward. It repeats the ancient watchword of the Church, *Sursum corda* : " Lift up your hearts." He Who said " I ascend," is also continually saying, " Follow Me." As the apostle puts it : " Set your affection on things above, where Christ sitteth at the right hand of God." In common talk, we use one short contemptuous adjective to brand things which we scorn and despise. A low story, a low trick, a low character—they stand for what good men must disdain. To set our mind on things higher and nobler, to cherish a lofty ideal of honour—this is what our fathers and mothers taught us, when they taught us to say our prayers. So St. Paul bids us rise above sordid aims and sensual pleasures and the ambition of the hour and the fashion of the crowd. There are modern prophets who wax fervent when they preach high thinking and devotion to the best. But the New Testament shows us what is that Best, on the summit of the universe. The first believers saw heaven opened, and for them the celestial spaces contained One Face and One Figure, in the midst of the eternal throne. They forgot all lesser and lower ideals, as they sang : " Thou art the King of glory, O Christ."

There is a movement in theology which claims to carry us " back to Christ." And we gain unspeakably because we are being brought face to face anew with the reality of the Word made flesh. We are taking in once more the actual human life and teaching and surroundings of the Son of God on earth. Yet we may miss the track in studying only the Lord's earthly history, even as pilgrims have gone astray who sought the holy sepulchre where once He lay buried, and those holy fields once trodden by His feet. To the primitive Church the cross was vacant, the tomb empty, the sky over Olivet a blank. " Back to Christ " should lead us not merely back to Bethlehem and Nazareth and Calvary, but up to Christ as He is now, crowned with glory and honour, at the right hand of God.

Christians often disobey the call *Sursum corda*, not from low secularity, but from perverted spirituality. We are tempted to set our mind on things within us. We gaze at the heart with its scars, we scrutinize the conscience with its stains, we question the memory with its chequered record—and we sink down into weariness and despair. The Gospel of the Ascension points us away, even from our own inward failures, up to Him Who has entered into the holiest, having obtained eternal redemption for us. It tells us that the issue of our salvation is not doubtful. Sin is defeated and vanquished, and the devil is a beaten foe. Jesus Christ has won the battle for us already, when He triumphed over the principalities and powers of darkness. And we have only by faith to gather up the fruits of His victory.

So, finally, the Ascension calls us away also from brooding over things around us—the corruptions and divisions in the Church, the cruelty and misery in the world—and points us upwards to Him Who holds them all, and their issues, in the hollow of His own pierced hand. It fixes our hearts on Him Who is sitting above the tumult of the people, Who must reign until He has subdued all things unto Himself. Surely to-day it needs no small act of faith, after we have finished reading the newspapers, to say, " Grace reigns,"—to be certain that Jesus Christ has overcome the world, and that the real mastery of things in heaven and of things on earth belongs to Him. Above all our defeat and disappointment and desolation, His voice out of the midst of the throne speaks the promise of His own victory to the humblest and feeblest of His disciples. " Where I am, there shall also My servant be." " Him that overcometh, I will give to him to sit down with Me in My throne."

THOU GOD SEEST ME

WE cannot tell how much the words meant to the outcast woman who murmured *Thou God seest me*, when the angel of the Lord found her, and Hagar knew that she was not forsaken in the wilderness. But for us, these four short words crystallize the soul of faith. As we ponder them, they grow more luminous and more profound. Here is one of those sayings which are elemental and universal; it penetrates below the surface of things and it goes down to the roots of religion. For real religion is born out of the sense of duty. Yet duty does not mean a vague instinct, or a code of inherited custom. Duty, to a Christian, is the consciousness that you are a person, and accountable to a supreme Person Who has the right to be obeyed. At the core of religion dwells this deep sense of being under God's authority and bound by God's will. A man is religious when he learns not only to say, " I ought," but to say " Thou hast made me, and Thou hast a claim on me." It is not safe to worship duty in the abstract. To satisfy our own conscience may turn into a subtle form of pleasing ourselves. To follow our inward light sometimes only means to canonize our private wilfulness. Conscience must be obeyed, indeed—not because it is naturally infallible, but because it is rectified and purified as the result of our obedience, so that it becomes, as we obey it, a mouthpiece to us of the Voice of God. The mandates of conscience borrow their awful majesty from Him Who is our Lover, our Redeemer, our Judge, Who speaks through the promptings of conscience and ratifies on our spirit its benedictions and its anathemas. For a Christian, the thought of Christ and the sense of His invisible Presence come to be like an external conscience, which purifies and corrects and heightens the natural instincts of right and wrong. The sanction of conscience resolves itself into this witness : *Thou God seest me.*

What a difference it makes to a man when first he grows aware that he is living under the personal scrutiny of His Maker. To begin with, it makes him honest and sincere. How often we try to conceal our real characters from ourselves. We refuse to examine the colour and quality of our motives ; the test is too painful ; we hate to look ourselves fairly in the face. But to know that God's pure gaze is always searching us through and through ; to feel that each lurking desire, each furtive resentment or regret, lies naked and open before the eyes of Him with Whom we have to do—this burning certainty shrivels up all our disguises and excuses. It helps to make us utterly honest and sincere in dealing with ourselves.

Again this fact *Thou God seest me*, steadily borne in mind, makes us humble. Nothing can properly cure a man of conceit and purge out that pride which infects us all—nothing but the sense of this ever-present, heart-piercing judgment of God. " What is God seeing in me to-day ? How do I show against His holiness ? What do I measure by His standard ? " No other questions have such power to keep us poor in spirit and to cleanse us from our secret sins.

In Russia the peasants have an *ikon*, the picture of some patron saint, hanging in every cottage. But there are times when a superstitious Russian will cover up his *ikon* with a cloth, so that the saint may not watch him while he is doing wrong. *Thou God seest me*— like the eye of a portrait on the wall which follows you wherever you go in the room. Is it no safeguard to recall the silent Spectator of every act, the unseen Listener at every conversation ? Moreover, if this truth curbs us, it also braces and fortifies the soul. Can I grow slack and careless, dare I scamp my work, while God is watching me all the time ? A craftsman often says of some idle apprentice : " I must put him where he will be under my own eye." And herein consists the divine discipline of character ; though no human sight observes us, we live and move and have our being ever in our great Taskmaster's eye.

Conversely, the same truth fortifies our self-respect—to know that our sins all lie naked before God, but before no one else except God. There are some confessions of the soul's dark secrets which become profane when made to any human ear ; if they be made, they relax and enfeeble the character. The evil of the confessional is that it discloses to another fallen creature what no fellow-being ought to see. A time comes when the penitent feels degraded to remember that confidence ; he repents that he ever betrayed himself, even to his nearest friend. But a man gains strength for recovery by the fact that his real self—the worst about him, as well as the best—is open to God only : God sees him, but God alone.

Moreover, this elemental truth, which humbles and rebukes and educates and strengthens, has power as well to interpret and to console. During my dreary and deserted years on earth, I know I am not forgotten in heaven. Men say about some old friend, " I have quite lost sight of him " ; but God does not lose sight of the least of His little ones, though no one else is looking after them in the whole world. A cynical proverb warns us that " out of sight is out of mind." But we can never sink out of God's sight, or lapse from His everlasting love. In this faith a man wins courage to toil on steadfastly, for the sake of something higher than recognition or reward. And so when a Christian finds himself misunderstood, when men misread his efforts and mock at his motives and sneer at his very sacrifice, he can appeal from human critics and censors to the only verdict which matters in the end : *Thou God seest me. Surely my judgment is with the Lord, and my work with my God.*

So amid our losses and disasters these words carry the secret of endurance and victory. God sees me, as one apart from all the dim multitudes of His children. God remembers me, on a solitary bed of pain. God has set His heart upon me, in my desolation. God has

His own purpose and hope even for my broken life. God is making something of my very suffering and weakness, according to His good pleasure. We have read the story of the crippled old Scotswoman, whose faith could triumph in this her favourite text. As she sat at her window in Thrums, she said : " I turn it up often, often, in the Bible. I read from the beginning of the chapter ; but when I come to *Thou God seest me* I stop, and let the Book lie in my lap—for once a body's sure of that, they're sure of all."

THE GREAT WHITE THRONE

AMID the overwhelming glories and terrors of the Apocalypse, there is one vision which fills our souls with serene and triumphant tranquillity. The prophet in exile who gazed upward and beheld the great white throne of heaven saw confronting him on earth the imperial throne of Cæsar—a throne blackened and bloodstained with Nero's nameless crimes. Yet high above human tyrants, above the rulers of the darkness of this world, he discerned by faith the One King, eternal, immortal, and invisible, reigning in stainless righteousness and love. Here is the supreme apocalypse of Scripture. Indeed, in a profound sense, the Bible from first to last may be described as the Book of the Revelation of the Great White Throne.

The Old Testament is taken up with this message. It sets out to teach and prove that justice belongs to the very nature of things, and governs all the corners of the universe. The Old Testament is continually proclaiming the holiness of God, affirming that He Who is Almighty is in His very being nothing but good and just. To us, this may sound like the mere alphabet of religion. But in ancient days the neighbours of Israel, the Moabites and the Sidonians, worshipped evil deities—such as tribes in tropical Africa worship now. They sacrificed to foul and monstrous idols, and paid homage to gods who were demons. Moreover, men had grown familiar with tyrants in human shape. The despots of primitive history governed by sheer wilfulness. For it is the essence of tyranny to act not according to right and justice, but by the tyrant's own caprice. To bondsmen who cowered before Sesostris or Sennacherib it seemed natural that they should bow down to a Sultan in the sky. And, therefore, the first lesson of revelation had to be this —that the Ruler of heaven and earth is pure and perfect goodness ; that the One Supreme Will loves righteousness and hates iniquity and avenges wrong ; that the Eternal Name is faithful and true. To modern Christians that doctrine appears an obvious postulate. But men had to learn through long generations of discipline that the throne of God must needs be " whiteness, most white." The revelation of the Gospel only deepened the awful reality of God's righteousness by disclosing in the midst of His throne a Lamb as it had been slain. The triumph-song of the redeemed rises into this climax : " Just and true are Thy ways, Thou King of saints." And the prayer which Christ Himself taught us ends with our confession of confidence in our Father, because the kingdom and the power and the glory are everlastingly His own.

This faith in the Great White Throne remains our final confession—the last refuge of all the perplexed and afflicted children of God. For still we see goodness despised and persecuted, and truth betrayed, and justice trampled underfoot. Still the embattled hosts of evil—thrones and dominations and principalities and powers—array themselves against the cause of right. How often our hearts rage in hot wrath against the cruelty and oppression in the world. How often, even in our own land, we discover that the weak are thrust aside because of their weakness, and the ignorant exploited by reason of their simplicity, and the poor defrauded and disinherited just because they are poor. There is only one assurance which can keep us brave to labour on for the least of Christ's little ones— the certainty that the Judge of all the earth shall avenge and recompense them at last.

So also, when the foes of the Church wax mighty, when its divisions multiply and its superstitions increase and all the legions of sin

and unbelief gather to assault the spiritual city,
where can timid Christians find refuge and
succour ? Faith has only one fortress : but
that is impregnable.

> " Under the shadow of Thy throne
>   Thy saints have dwelt secure."

For there, and there alone, do they begin
to understand the solemn prophecy against
God's enemies : " The kings of the earth set
themselves, and the rulers take counsel together,
against the Lord, and against His anointed . . .
He that sitteth in the heavens shall laugh : the
Lord shall have them in derision."

Even in days of dreadful conflict and massacre,
when men's hearts grow sick at the news of
horrors which they dare not describe, Christians
cling fast to their confidence in the King of righteousness. When each morning brings word of
fresh bloodshed, we fall back upon the faith of
the martyrs. For every martyrdom on earth
makes mute appeal to the Supreme Arbiter
and the Last Assize. Every brave life laid
down for the sake of truth and freedom cries
out for the recompense of God. And though as
men count time God's answer tarries, it is
already written and registered in heaven.

> " Martyrs, what of the night ?
>   Nay, is it night with you yet ?
>   We—for our part—we forget
>   What night was, if it were.
>   The loud red mouths of the fight
>   Are silent and shut where we are.

In our eyes the tempestuous air
  Shines as the face of a star."

The faith of the martyrs has been the same in all ages. They have endured their agony, as seeing the Invisible. Above the world's darkness and rebellion they caught the shining vision of the Great White Throne. We learn the secret of their sweetness and patience and fortitude when we cast ourselves before the Throne and before the Lamb, when we submit our spirits as dear children to His holy and awful Will, and enter into His rest. So, amid wars and rumours of wars, even we may possess that victorious peace which passeth all understanding. For the Lord of hosts hath established His throne in the heavens ; and *His kingdom ruleth over all*.

LAID UP IN THE ARK

THE tabernacle which Moses made in the wilderness was a pavilion, curtained off into two chambers. First came the holy place, with its golden table for shewbread, its golden altar for incense, and its golden lampstand for light. Beyond this outer sanctuary lay the most holy place. Behind its veil no man might pass except the high priest, and he but once a year. Within there stood " the ark of the covenant overlaid round about with pure gold, wherein was the golden pot that had manna, and Aaron's rod that budded, and the tables of the covenant ;

and over it the cherubims of glory shadowing the mercy seat." How much this sacred ark meant to primitive Israelites, it is hard for us to realize now. In their eyes it was the actual dwelling-place of God's presence, the shrine where His glory brooded and from which His grace and His mercy flowed. And so the ark came to be looked upon as the palladium of the Hebrew people, the visible symbol with which their faith and their fortunes were bound up. In the Book of Judges we have glimpses of stormy and lawless times when the ark wandered hither and thither—now hurried into battle and lost, and again brought back from captivity. Such episodes remind us of the dark ages of Christendom, when monks fled into exile carrying with them their chest of sacred relics which had mysterious power to curse and to bless.

Regarding the actual relics which were treasured up in the ark of Israel, we know certainly of three—the pot of manna, the rod that budded, and the tables of the covenant. The omer full of manna had been laid up before the Lord in memory of that bread which came down from heaven, when God spread a table in the wilderness and men did eat angels' food. Concerning the rod that budded, we read that when jealousy broke out between the Hebrew tribes, the prince of each tribe handed a rod to Moses, who laid them together before the Lord in the tabernacle of witness. And on the morrow, out of these twelve, the rod of Aaron

for the tribe of Levi was found to have blossomed
—like the pilgrim staff of Tannhäuser in the
medieval legend ; the bare dead wood showed
leaf and flower, as a token from God to signify
which tribe He had chosen. Finally, laid up in
the ark were the tables of the covenant, inscribed with the Commandments. Those slabs
of stone came down from the granite peaks of
Sinai, where the Law had been spoken in
thunder, and graven thereon by no mortal
finger were the Ten Words of God's will. No
relic could be more venerable, more precious.
Israel's law of duty sank so deep into the
conscience of mankind that to this very day
we find it written on the walls of our churches.
The Commandments sum up the earliest revelation, never to be superseded : *I am the Lord
thy God . . . thou shalt have no other gods before
Me.*

The ancient ark suffered many changes and
vicissitudes. It had been opened and searched
by profane hands, before it found a home
finally in the sanctuary of Solomon's temple.
But when the priests carried it there to its rest,
they lifted the lid to look for the last time at
what lay therein ; and we read " there was
nothing in the ark, save the two tables of stone
which Moses put there at Horeb." Other relics
had disappeared ; but there remained what
seemed like a fragment of the Rock of Ages,
bearing witness to the imperishable law of duty.

" Now these things are an allegory," concerning the true tabernacle which the Lord hath pitched and not man. We follow the spirit of the Epistle to the Hebrews when we apply them to the holy of holies which each man carries hidden in his own breast. Physiologists tell us of a law according to which the experience of each individual reproduces the life-history of the race. And this law also has its spiritual analogue. What do we keep laid up in our personal ark? What are those possessions which nothing could replace if we lost them? Suppose—to imagine the impossible—some modern mother in Israel consented to unlock her own private reliquary and exhibit its contents, what should we find treasured there? Perhaps an old-fashioned miniature; a bundle of yellow letters; a bit of needlework which dear hands left unfinished, which will never be finished now; a tress of hair, with the sunshine faded out of its gold; a pair of baby's shoes; a tiny Testament, with dim writing on the fly-leaf; a thin, worn wedding-ring; two copper coins, once laid on the eyelids of the dead. Relics like these, worthless in themselves, can be beyond price to a tender, loyal, unforgetting heart. Of all fragrant herbs which grow in life's garden, none is like rosemary, as Ophelia knew: *There's rosemary—that's for remembrance.*

And, passing beyond material tokens to inward recollections, what is it that you treasure in the ark of memory—in the soul's secret chamber, " remote, occult, withdrawn " ? In the shrine and reliquary of the heart—what is laid up there ? Pray God that it may be indeed a holy place, from which dark and bitter thoughts are banished, where no rancour and revenge are lurking. Divine grace has power to cleanse and sweeten even our memories. And if the heart, like the ancient ark of Israel, be indeed abiding under the shadow of the wings of God, it cannot hold anything but tenderness and forgiveness and praise. Search and see what is stored therein, deeper than all beside. Have you not what seems like manna, a trophy of God's providence ? Have you no recollection of how He Himself fed your hunger with bread from heaven, and satisfied your longing soul with love ? Again, is there nothing to correspond with the rod that budded ? Remember how God quickened your dull, dry spirit with new life and hope, and how that very quickening became the token of His choice. Your election to service was proved by that fresh vital energy. You knew that He had called you, by the fact that your whole being thrilled with the life that is life indeed.

Look again into the ark of memory. It holds something still earlier in experience, something which is far more awful and more enduring. Is there not a law of duty, graven on fleshy tables of the heart ? Is there not a primeval covenant made between yourself and your Maker ? This is the first and the last and the

16

changeless fact, over which in spite of all changes the soul shuts fast. At the end of the day there may be nothing left but this. But in the deep secret of experience each servant of God cherishes this word, *Thou shalt have no other gods before Me.* Whatever else he loses, he carries a covenant in his heart—the covenant which binds him in life and death to the faithfulness of his King.

GOD'S ARITHMETIC

THE Bible is the text-book of the divine calculus. In the Psalter we find one application of God's arithmetic : " Thou tellest the number of the stars ; He calleth them all by their names. . . . When I consider Thy heavens, the work of Thy fingers, the moon and the stars which Thou hast ordained ; what is man, that Thou art mindful of him ? and the son of man, that Thou visitest him ? " That ancient question still creeps into the hearts of Christians. We feel the same overwhelming contrast between God's universe and the human creatures whom He visits and redeems. Perhaps we feel it now more acutely than men of old. The Psalmist was a mere star-gazer on the hill-sides, watching the sky as he tended his flock by night. To him the moving firmament was glorious and wonderful, but it turned round the earth as its centre. The lights in the firmament existed for man's sake, set there to be signs for him and

seasons.   Whereas, when we consider the
heavens now, we have learnt to weigh and
measure the burning lamps above us, we can
peer into the awful gulfs far beyond.   For us,
this solid earth has shrivelled into the least of
little wandering stars, and the sun himself is a
lonely pilgrim across the waste places of the
sky.   We feel dazed and lost amid unfathomable spaces, sprinkled with innumerable worlds
beyond our ken.   Is it not a staggering thought
that our human planet should be the object of
God's love and the theatre of God's redemption ?   How can the Maker and Master of such
a universe vex Himself over the puny lives of
men ?

Now to such a question there must be some
kind of answer, if faith and goodness are to
keep alive.   For the question cuts the nerve
of practical morality.   This freezing doubt
paralyses conscience.   A universe so boundless
dwarfs us into self-contempt.   Whenever a man
comes to believe that he is not worth God's
care, he will soon go on to believe that he is
not worth his own care.   Even to himself he
will appear too paltry, too fugitive, for any
serious end or effort.   Why should he trouble ?
In a little time, good and evil will end together,
and nothing will be any longer worth while.

Yet after all, is there not something grandiose
about the marvels of popular astronomy ?
When we listen to the sounding tale of material
vastness, we reflect that this is only so much

dead matter after all. Even though God has
been pleased to kindle so many more billion
tons of hydrogen in one corner of the universe
than in another, need we therefore lose our
spiritual balance or despise our own souls?
Fill all the corners of space with incandescent
vapour, and the whole of it is not worthy to be
compared with one of the Psalms of David.

Moreover, the discoverer who considers and
observes the heavens must be somehow greater,
and not less, than those spaces and masses
which he has learned how to gauge. On any
reasonable estimate, an astronomer like Sir
William Herschel must out-value the great
nebula in Orion, which he resolved and depicted.
When we gaze at that vast work of God's fingers
we can still go on to say, " What a piece of work
is a man ! " The very fact that we are able
to ask the Psalmist's question with added
emphasis and deeper meaning, shows that we
ourselves, who ask it, constitute part of the
reply.

Imagination breaks down and refuses to
compare things which have no common measure
—like a child and a star. But our human hearts
rise up and affirm out of their very nature and
instinct that the starry universe is small dust
in the balance, weighed against truth and
loyalty and love and sacrifice. For things like
these are of another order and quality, they
belong to the absolute region which transcends
all mortal time and space. The Gospel reveals

as its central fact that self-sacrifice is the very nature of God : and that is an absolute fact—true in the farthest corners of creation, valid when earth and sun and stars are gathered up like a garment that waxes old and vanishes away.

The truth of this comes home to us in hours of insight, which are also our keenest hours of rapture or of pain. When we conquer some strong temptation, when we suffer some great betrayal, when we risk our all in a righteous cause, when we stand by the grave where our treasure lies under seals of clay—then, in the depths of experience, we become aware that the things that are seen are temporal and the things that are not seen are eternal.

The Gospel gives us another application of God's arithmetic. Our Lord Himself did not use arguments to refute our human sense of insignificance. He simply affirmed the Eternal Fatherhood, whose nature He Himself revealed ; and He declared that even the least and lowest of God's children is unspeakably precious in God's eyes. We dread to be lost in the wilderness of empty space ; or we shiver lest we drop out of sight as of no account among myriads of souls. But our thoughts about things mean and things mighty are not God's thoughts ; our ways of despising the common and trivial are not God's ways. *He telleth the number of the stars, He calleth them all by their names. . . . He calleth His own sheep by name. . . . The very hairs of your head are all numbered.*

I am poor and needy, yet the Lord thinketh upon me. I am stained and sinful, yet the Lord forgiveth me. I am foolish and perplexed, yet the Lord guideth me. I am lonely and forsaken, yet the Lord remembereth me. I am sorrowful and sick at heart, yet the Lord loveth me. The very hairs of my head are all numbered—those hairs which trouble has whitened, they are numbered by my God. All that I am, all that I possess, all that I have passed through —my training and temperament, my health and home, my friends and kinsfolk, my sins and shames, my hopes and dreams—Lo, O Lord, Thou knowest them altogether.

The steps of my feet are all numbered, and the tears of my trouble, and the sighs of my desiring. Innumerable evils have compassed me about ; but they are all numbered. Mine iniquities have taken hold upon me, so that I am not able to look up ; they are more than the hairs of mine head, therefore my heart faileth me ; but they are all numbered, and atoned for, and blotted out, and put away. And the beats of my pulse are all numbered. God knows how many grains of sand are left to run out of the glass before He gives me that marching order for a better country which no soul can disobey.

Whatever strange worlds open beyond death's gateway, through whatever spaces of the unseen the soul may hereafter wander, it shall not be a soul lost and homeless and forgotten in the wilderness of eternity, but a soul remembered and redeemed and purified and at home—in a place prepared for it in the personal love of God.

HE CALLETH HIS SHEEP BY NAME

THE men who tend the flocks to-day on a Scottish moor or an Australian sheep-run are seldom shepherds after the pattern pictured in the Bible. Now, they generally think of their sheep as livestock—so much flesh, and so many fleeces. But on the hill-sides of Syria when the world was young, a shepherd's life and a shepherd's thoughts were different. Then he lived mostly alone, with his sheep for company. There were savage beasts he must guard them against, and more savage men. There were green pastures and springs of water that he must seek out and lead them to. Such experiences of peril and hardship and solitude naturally drew a shepherd into curious fellow-feeling for the dumb creatures he had in charge. The great wilderness, where nature is so overwhelming and human beings are so rare, made him forget the gulf between the man and the brute. Gradually his sheep would become to him like companions, almost like friends. One of the vivid touches in *Robinson Crusoe* describes how Crusoe's loneliness drove him to make friends with the animals he caught and tamed. So we can understand how—just as a whipper-in to-day knows every hound in the pack, and calls

them by name—just as a groom knows every
horse in the stud, and calls them by name—a
primitive shepherd knew each sheep in the
flock ; he cared about them because he had
risked and spent himself for their sakes ; and
he had a separate name for them every one.

Such was the bond of sympathy to which our
Lord pointed in His parable. The Shepherd
of the souls of men remembers us, one by one.
He cares for each of us with a separate solicitude,
He has given Himself for each of us with a
personal sacrifice—as though in the whole
world's wilderness there were no other but that
single one.

When we try to answer the question " What's
in a name ? " we remember that each Englishman has at least two names—his surname,
which comes to him as the member of a family,
and his Christian name, which belongs to him
as an individual person. In old pagan days
when a heathen was converted and brought
into the Church, he renounced his old name
with his old life, he became a new man, and at
his baptism he received a new name. And
later, when a child was brought to be baptized,
it received the name which it was to bear as
one of God's children. That baptismal or
Christian name marked the human creature as
an immortal being—it was the name he was to
be known by as solemnly consecrated to God.
Whereas the surname, as the word implies, was
originally an addition to the other.   Sometimes

it was a patronymic, or a trade-name, or a nick-
name ; but essentially it was something extra.
By means of certain legal formalities a man can
change his surname ; but his Christian name
clings to him like the seal of his very self.   In
like manner, the name by which Christ calls me
is no mere chance word or catch-word ; it is
my real name which I cannot escape, which
I cannot deny, the name which no alias can
abolish, the name which stands for my identity
in the creation of God.

Moreover, a man's Christian name was also
his distinctive name, by which he was marked
out and separated from the rest of his family.
In earlier ages it seemed natural to regard men
as grouped in kindreds and tribes.   Society in
primitive times was not what we assume it to
be now—a collection of individuals ; it was an
aggregation of families.   A man's individuality
was lost among his kinsfolk.   Nothing in ancient
history is more pathetically impressive than the
way in which human beings move across the
stage in vast, dim, uncounted multitudes.   The
individual was swallowed up and forgotten in
his caste, his tribe, his nation.   He did not
properly exist as a person, until Christ came and
called him by name.   And to-day, when armies
are marshalled by millions, when the unit seems
lost in the aggregate, we still need the warning
of the Son of Sirach : " Say not thou, I will
hide myself from the Lord, I shall not be remembered among so many people.   For what

is my soul among such an infinite multitude of
creatures ? "

The name by which Christ calls you—your
Christian name—gives you that sense of personality without which we are not men at all.
It brings home to you your separate accounta-
bility, it marks you out as a creature of infinite
preciousness in the eyes of God. Christ calls
each of us by a particular name, because He
loves each of us with a special affection, He
thinks about each of us with a peculiar care,
He brings us face to face with Himself singly, one
by one. Christ's word comes indeed to all,
like the order given to a regiment, like the lesson
taught to a class. But that word comes besides
to each solitary man, and isolates him from his
fellows, and makes him lonely in the midst of a
great company. It names him by name, and
searches his conscience, and whispers in his
heart, " Where art thou ? "

Finally a man's Christian name not only
stands for his personal identity and his individual
responsibility, it is also his familiar and endear-
ing name. Amid life's common business the
people we mix with call us by our surname—
the title of respect and formality and reserve.
But in our own homes and with our dearest
friends, when reserve is forgotten and affection
is free, we are called by our Christian name.
Often you date your intimacy with a man from
the day when you could venture to use his
familiar name. So gracious, so intimate, so en-

dearing is the call of Jesus Christ. He speaks not as to a stranger or a servant, but as to a familiar friend. He calls me by the name which marks me for His own possession—the object of His eternal thought, His awful choice, His quenchless desire, His unspeakable passion. *He telleth the number of the stars ; He calleth them all by their names.* But the same Voice reaches the most forlorn among the children of men, and calls him by that name by which his mother used to call him, and claims him by love and sacrifice which are far beyond a mother's : " Fear thou not, for I have redeemed thee, I have called thee by thy name ; thou art Mine."

All through the war the Eternal Shepherd has been calling multitudes of our soldiers each one by name out of the midst of battle, calling our bravest and dearest home to Himself. Here on earth men write them down as fallen : but the angels whisper that they are risen indeed. In this dark world they have left us desolate and empty-hearted. Yet we have still faith to be among the patient companies that watch for the morning ; we are still able to give thanks for those whom we love, to whom Christ has called one by one, saying : " Arise thou, and come away."

I WILL BE TO THEM A GOD

ONE ruling idea which runs through the Bible is the idea of a covenant between God and His

people. In after ages the name, and the
thought which it expressed, passed into the
marrow of Puritan faith. The Puritans made
a solemn league and covenant with one another,
because they knew that they had entered
already into a covenant with God which was
more solemn still. Our own fathers and grand-
fathers were familiar with the sound of that
word covenant : it echoed through the sermons
and the hymns which they loved best. And on
the title-page of Scripture we still read *The Holy
Bible, containing the Old and New Testaments,*
where Testament is just another name for
Covenant. " The writings of the New Covenant " was the title by which the Gospels and
Epistles collectively were known to the primitive
Church. The first Christians realized that
those writings constituted the very bonds and
indentures of their fellowship in Christ Jesus.
For the Christian sense of the word covenant
suggests not a legal document or a mercantile
bargain, but a moral and spiritual bond. It
means more than an agreement or compact ;
it implies an alliance and a partnership as well.
Marriage may be taken as the cardinal instance
of a covenant made between two human souls
—ratified by public vows, but in its essence a
spiritual pledge and troth-plighting, for richer,
for poorer, for better, for worse. The covenant
between God and man is to be thought of as a
bond of similar order and quality—not formal,
artificial, temporary, but rooted in the very

nature of things, inscribed in our minds and engraven on our hearts—and sealed by the holiest of sanctions, by the blood of the everlasting covenant.

Rousseau's theory of a " Social Contract " was a fiction. Yet even that fiction points to an immense truth. Each of us is born into a strange web of relationships, which he did not fashion, which he can never renounce or escape. From our infancy we are linked with other lives and knit up with other hearts. The bonds of blood and the ties of kindred and country are chosen and woven for us. In his family, in his business, in his town, in his native land, every man finds himself daily beset with imperious duties and entangled among sacred irrevocable claims. In this deep sense we are all children of the great human covenant. And it is required of us that we be found faithful.

For the very idea of a covenant demands that it be loyally kept. Two voices of exhortation are ringing through Scripture. The first voice bids us have faith, and the second voice bids us keep faith. To have faith is the seed of religion ; to keep faith is the flower and fruit of religion. Our trust is justified, in so far as it makes us trustworthy. Plain people understand how precious is this simple humdrum virtue of fidelity. No virtue ranks higher in the practical conduct of life. In business and in friendship we discover in the end how much better than any amount of cleverness is absolute reliability. When you find the man whom you can always entirely depend upon, so that to trust him is like resting against a rock, that man's price is above rubies. We admire the brilliant engaging people, we respond to their charm of manner, we recognize their touch of genius. But whenever trouble comes, we turn by instinct to the dull commonplace men or the quiet homely women, who have no shining gifts except this simple, incomparable virtue of never failing in their obligations and never breaking their word. A faithful son, a faithful brother, a faithful friend, a faithful partner, a faithful servant—these are the folk whom we really lean upon and value and honour. We bless God for them while they are with us ; and we miss them irreparably when He takes them away.

The preciousness of fidelity comes home to us when we suffer from its defect, when we are disappointed and deceived by someone in whom we had placed implicit confidence. We begin then to realize that the basest of all crimes was summed up in the words, " who also betrayed Him." Civilized life becomes impossible when men break covenant with one another. Human law exists to enforce the sacredness of covenants, and that sacredness is affirmed and guarded in the most ancient code of divine law. When we hear the Ten Commandments read in church, we often miss the point of the precept : " Thou shalt not take the name of the Lord thy God

in vain." Those words do not simply prohibit
profane swearing. In early ages men ratified
their covenants with one another by invoking
the awful name of God ; and to take God's name
in vain meant breaking the covenant which
that name had consecrated. The Lord will not
hold men guiltless—or nations guiltless—who
break their solemn covenants.

Such thoughts as these concerning the simple
old-fashioned duty of keeping faith one with
another point us on towards the duty of keeping
faith with Him to Whom we belong by the
covenant of our creation and our redemption.
To Him we are personally responsible, and to
Him we must give strict and solemn account at
last. Our Lord judges us by our fidelity to the
individual charge which He has committed into
our hands and trusted us to keep. He scruti-
nizes, not our success, but our steady patient
loyalty to the obligations which He has laid
upon our consciences. And Christ Himself can
speak no higher praise than this : " Well done,
thou good and faithful servant, enter thou into
the joy of thy Lord." When we do enter therein,
we shall discover that it is the joy of Him Who
was Himself found utterly faithful, even unto
death—that death in which He finished the
work given Him to do.

Finally we may remind ourselves that a
covenant, from the nature of the case, must be
a mutual thing. In heaven, as well as on earth,
it binds both parties ; and therefore this is the

formula of the new covenant : " I will be to
them a God, and they shall be to me a people."
It is God that hath made us, and He is a faithful
Creator. He cannot deny Himself. He will be
to us a God. His Fatherhood is a living tie
which it is not possible for Him to break. It
is the glory of God to be the faithful Father,
striving to save to the uttermost. This is the
God whom Christ has made real to the world.
He shows us God doing what it is natural for
His fidelity to do—God recognizing the burden
of His Fatherhood towards every human
creature—God bearing all things and enduring
all things for the sake of those whom He can
never give up, because they are His own. If
faithfulness is the deepest virtue in man, then
we can rely on the utter faithfulness of Him
who having loved His own, loves them unto the
end.

This is what the Puritans meant when they
spoke of a covenant-keeping God.

Such a covenant implies fixity and security.
It is ordered in all things and sure. It lies
deeper than our fluctuations of feeling and
moods of emotion, it endures through the
chances and changes of outward affairs. God
has bound us to Himself by links which are
settled and stablished beyond our altering.
Though we be faithless, He abideth faithful.
Not in ourselves, but in Thee, O Lord, have we
trusted ; let us never be confounded : we
never shall be—we never can.

St. Paul does not scruple to commandeer military phrases and figures of speech, and to enlist them for expressing his own fiery zeal. When he exhorted Timothy to *fight the good fight of faith*, he was writing to a missionary, not to a soldier. And while his words thrill us like the notes of a bugle, they come home to every true-hearted Christian, whether he be serving in the army or not. Certainly such words mean more to us to-day than they meant once. Whatever else may be true about the war, it has assuredly brought to light the one profound and fundamental cleavage which runs through the world and sets men asunder. We perceive now that the supreme controversy is not between wrangling sects : it is between those who think that there is nothing worth living for but life itself, and those who think that life is worth nothing unless it is lived well. Must a man live for a more or less enlightened self-interest ? Or can he live so that he may forget himself altogether in those things which he can love for their own sake ? Here is the decisive question—the only question which finally matters. All who answer in one way are in one camp, and all who answer in the opposite way are arrayed in the other camp— and the two are eternally hostile. The martial phrases of the Bible ring with fresh life and meaning, as we feel to-day that there is a real

17   257

unfaith, a spiritual devilry to be fought—and there is no discharge in this war.

Half our confusion in regard to faith grows out of the notion that faith is concerned with things ; whereas faith is not concerned with things at all, it is concerned with persons. Faith really means your personal confidence in some other person, your reliance on the character of another. You are faithful to an old friend when you go on trusting him, even though men suspect him and slander him ; when you rely on his honour in spite of ugly circumstances and damaging reports. You know he will never forget you, or betray you, or desert you, or give you away. He may be out of sight in a far country, but you dare stake your life that he is a true man and no traitor. Even though things look black against him, though at times you yourself are inclined to misjudge him and feel tempted to suspect him, still if you are a loyal friend you struggle against such base doubts, you trample on your suspicions and cast them away. You trust your friend in the teeth of appearances. You defend his good name, you fight for his honour.

Friendship supplies a key to the secrets of religion. Faith in God means that though He is out of sight, I trust His personal goodness ; I rely on His fidelity ; I know He will keep His word. Many things which God does, I cannot understand ; why He suffers some things to be done in the world, I cannot explain. But I know that God's Heart is nothing but pure and perfect goodness. Though all men be selfish, God is Love ; and He is true though every man be a liar. When other people doubt God and reproach Him and deny Him, I cling to Him in the dark : for He cannot deny Himself. Even though I be tempted to doubt Him, I fling doubt and suspicion away ; I venture on God in the teeth of appearances ; I champion His Name and His honour. Herein is part of what it means to fight the good fight of faith.

In this confused and tragic world we need not miss our way if we regard it from the point of view of the Bible as one great battlefield where good and evil are perpetually at war. The eternal struggle between right and wrong is going on everywhere, not only in trenches and billets and barrack-rooms, but in every work-shop and every market-place, in our own homes and in our hearts. Sometimes it looks as though the good cause were going to be beaten, as though selfishness really did pay best in the end. But a faithful soldier knows that in this endless conflict between light and darkness God Almighty Himself is on the side of right, and so the right side must prove the winning side at last.

Why is the good fight called good ? This word " good " properly means gallant, noble, glorious—the fight which it is worth a man's life not to miss. Some persons maintain, indeed, that good is another name for profitable, it means something that is worth doing because it pays so well. But true-hearted fighting men never argue in the spirit of the huckster. Very few of our soldiers enlisted because they could make more money by enlisting. There were other persons who stayed behind in order to make money ; but the true men heard their country calling them in her danger and they rose up and went—though it cost them so much. They went gallantly, because they knew in their hearts that it was good to go. They have left us all a lesson about what Milton called " something more high and heroical in religion." Faith means not only accepting the unspeakable gift : it means hazarding the unspeakable venture.

In the everlasting war between love and selfishness, Christ calls us to fight on His side. He does not promise us easy service, or sumptuous rations, or wealthy pay ; but He makes us understand that to fight this battle with Him is the finest and noblest and most glorious thing in the world—the one thing worth living for. To choose this is to choose the only part that deserves to be called good, the part that is so good because it shall never be taken away. To refuse it is to miss the very prize and crown of life.

After Napoleon's most amazing victory in Italy, he caused a medal to be struck for his soldiers who fought and conquered in that wonderful conflict. On the reverse of the medal was the name *Marengo* : the obverse showed only these proud words, *I was there*.

LET NO MAN TAKE THY CROWN

ON the walls of the Chapel of the Arena at Padua, Giotto has painted the chief vices and virtues of men. One of his great frescoes there is a picture of Hope, and this is how he imagines her. Hope is drawn as a woman, white-robed and white-winged ; her eyes are gazing upward, and she stretches out her hands to grasp the crown which an angel holds just above her reach. According to the definition of a modern English prophet, hope is that temper or virtue in us which answers to and embraces great and worthy things hoped for. And the old Italian artist symbolized the eager attitude of soul, the heavenward expectancy, concerning which St. Paul declares that *we are saved by hope*. For Christian hope implies a high and noble ideal, a crown beyond our grasp at present, which is yet to be reached out after continually and to be gained in the end. In all generations men have asked themselves what is the supreme ideal to strive for ? What is the prize which they ought to set before themselves as the one object to attain ? The Christian answer is not doubtful, even if it seem " dark with excess of light." Christ has told us plainly that the crown of human existence is to be conformed to Himself ; to become like Him, because we see Him as He is ; to be made pure as He is pure ; to be without selfishness, without envy, without pride ; to live altogether in the peace and joy and love of God, and of those who are like God—and so to live for ever. This is the crown which the angel is holding out above our reach. So divine an ideal appears too high for us ; but the Bible sets forth plainly what God intends man's life to become. To grow like Jesus Christ, to have our characters transformed into the image of His character, until we love what He loves and we hate what He hates and we dwell as He dwells in the bosom of God—this is the glorious hope held out to us in the Gospel. And the virtue and blessing of such a hope come from living day by day in the light of its glory—a glory which shall be revealed even in us.

Among men who would take away our crown, there are some who try to tarnish it and cheapen it ; they cry it down as mere pinchbeck, and not pure gold. There are critics who denounce our Christian hope as covetous and selfish. In truth the Gospel may sometimes be perverted into a sort of bribe or appeal to mere self-interest, when people are urged to be virtuous on earth because their reward shall be great in heaven. Yet the very quality of the Christian ideal forbids any man to seek it selfishly. The essence of the crown of life is to become as self-forgetful as Christ Himself. Our Lord lifts us out of self-seeking here and now, by the

promise that we shall be made perfectly un-
selfish at last. And the assurance of hope lies
in this—that what we look for is even now
beginning by God's grace to come true in our
souls. His Spirit is the earnest of our inheritance ; and the foretaste of blessing which we
possess makes us bold to look forward to that
full beatitude waiting for us in the end.

In Giotto's fresco, consider the eager attitude
in which Hope is standing. Before any man
can be saved by hope, there must be more than
a vision of the crown : there must be a heart
that hungers and longs for it, there must be
hands that drop all else to grasp it, there must
be eyes whose gaze is so fastened on it that they
let other sights go by. And when we think
seriously about the destiny of man, we begin to
understand what is, and what is not, immortally
worth while. God has set before our spirits
this supreme object—that we should be more
and more filled with His love and more and
more conformed to His Son, until at last there
is nothing at all left in us which is not His own.
To realize such a hope as this redeems us from
half our temptations ; it disentangles us from
the world ; it lends us wings which lift and
bear the drooping soul. In this sense we are
saved by hope.

The antipodes of hope is despair—despair of
ourselves, or of our fellow-creatures, or of God's
universe. We are doomed and ruined by
despair. Yet which of us has never been

tempted to give up hoping ? He has made such countless failures ; he is standing amid broken vows and haunting sins. Many a man who set out on the narrow way in faith and hope after a while desponds and recoils. The ideal seems too transcendent : it is high, he cannot attain unto it. Nothing but God's own Spirit can kindle us with fresh courage in the midst of our despondency. He alone can reveal the crown of life, far above us, but still possible for us— yea, reserved for us in spite of all our past. And the test of hope is to be obedient to this heavenly vision through years of drudgery and obscurity, to acquiesce in nothing lower or meaner, to let no dullness and languor of spirit make us content with less than what Christ Himself set before us on that day when He bowed our hearts to obey His own sweet imperious call, *Follow thou Me.*

After all, the error of the optimist is trifling compared with the falsehood of the pessimist. Our Christian hope can be entirely optimist, according to God's standard of what is best. But that does not make us confident that out- ward forms are permanent, or that earthly institutions are essential. In spite of wars and rumours of wars our hope for the universe would stand unshattered though God shake not the earth only, but also heaven. Nay, this immortal hope in the purpose of predestinating Love is only purified through much tribulation.

We may well lay to heart the saying of an

eloquent American bishop : " The power of any life lies in its expectancy." What are we hoping for ? What do we expect, in our highest dreams ? The answer to these questions is the measure of the degree in which we are indeed living. When a man can answer them as St. Paul did, and can say, " The Lord is at hand ; I am expecting a higher, deeper, more perfect mastery of Christ. I am hoping to grow more and more into His goodness "— that man is alive indeed. The prize that Christians strive for is spoken of as the crown of life, because the essence of its blessing is to become day by day more vitally and more abundantly alive—in the life of God.

THE WORK OF THINE OWN HANDS

THE chapel of San Lorenzo at Florence contains the monuments which Michael Angelo executed in memory of the Medici, his princely patrons. On one of these tombs the sculptor has carved two reclining figures, to represent respectively the Night and the Day. Night is personified as a woman, sunk in deep yet uneasy slumber ; while Day is portrayed in the shape of a man who lifts himself in the attitude of wrathful and disturbed awakening. But the figure of Day has been left unfinished. The limbs indeed are partly chiselled, while the head and face are merely blocked out of the marble. Some interruption stayed the master's hand, and he left his work imperfect and incomplete. Now that half-finished statue in San Lorenzo is like a parable of our human nature. There is the same pathetic sense of incompleteness, the same dumb prophecy of a perfection intended and required. The sculptor's ideal seems vainly struggling to free itself from its stony shroud ; and the marble lips might cry out in mute reproach, beseeching him to perfect that which concerned them, to forsake not the work of his own hands.

In the frame and fabric of things, as we see them in the world without us and as we know them within our own hearts, there appears a strange incompleteness, which waits to be made perfect. Every good thing in our experience is the work of God's good Spirit. Our very shame and remorse, no less than our penitence and pardon and peace, are wrought out within us by the operation of the grace of God. From first to last the Christian experience is super-natural—the repair of our weakness by Divine strength, the supply of our emptiness out of Divine bounty. And this very fact becomes the ground and rock on which Christian confidence is founded. Because, as a great preacher once declared, " It is not God's way to do things by halves." The good work which He has begun in us is not finished yet. But even now we can understand something of what He means it to become ; and though the will of God be interrupted, it is never finally abandoned. Not seldom an earthly artist can be hindered or distracted from his task. Sometimes he will fling down the tools in impatience and despair. Old age must paralyse his hand in a few years at most. But the Divine Worker fainteth not, neither is weary. His patience is like His mercy, it endureth for ever ; and He has all eternity to finish in. Sometimes we describe a man by comparing him to a rough diamond. And that surely implies that his character needs a great deal of cutting and grinding and polishing. But it means also that God the Owner sees something in that man which is worth taking infinite pains over—something which He will never " cast as rubbish to the void," but will go on to discipline through much tribulation until He has made it at last what He means it to be.

It is not God's way to do things by halves. Our confidence for ourselves and for all mankind is simply a falling back upon our Lord's eternal fidelity. His patience never grows tired. His love never wears out. In some of us faith itself often seems a crippled and broken thing ; but He is faithful Who has suffered and conquered for our sakes, He is faithful Who has promised and Who died to keep His word. Since time began Christ has never yet disappointed or betrayed the humblest creature who trusted Him. When once He has begun a good work in a soul, He will surely purify and perfect that soul in the end.

It is not God's way to do things by halves. When we think how much He has done in us already and how far He has brought us, we dare not permit ourselves to doubt Him for days and years to come. We dare not dream that He will desert us when we need Him most, or that He will make demands on us that we cannot render, or that He will in any wise forsake the work of His own hands. Faithful is He that calleth us, Who also will do it. And that which He has done already is only the pledge and promise of what He will yet perform. To Him, as to a faithful Creator, we can commit the keeping of our bodies and souls, alike for things present and for things to come. O Lord, in Thee have we trusted—not in our own vows or our own perseverance, but in Thee. Forsake not the work of Thine own hands.

WAR IN HEAVEN

A MESSAGE FOR MICHAELMAS

To many people Michaelmas suggests no more than the end of summer and a quarter-day for accounts. We hardly stop to remember that it was so called because on that day Western Christendom celebrated the festival of St. Michael and all angels. The Bible tells us little about the nature and powers of these spiritual beings, whose functions seem often to dwarf their personality. Yet our Lord's own words in the Gospels acknowledge distinctly that angels are real, and not any mere figure of speech. In the book of Daniel the name Michael is given to a chief of the heavenly host, who is styled " prince " or guardian angel of Israel ; and in Jewish speculation he appears as the greatest of them all, first of the four who surround the throne of God. The New Testament refers to him as the supreme spirit of good triumphing over evil. Nothing less can be implied by the tremendous text in the Apocalypse : *There was war in heaven : Michael and his angels fought against the dragon.*

" War in heaven " sounds like an utter contradiction. Yet the Gospel delights to express itself in paradox. Many of Christ's most penetrating sayings were spoken as paradoxes. The character which He demands and which He creates is described by a series of apparent contradictions—hungry, and yet satisfied ; meek, yet inheriting the earth ; humble, yet receiving the kingdom ; sorrowful, yet always rejoicing ; poor, yet making many rich ; having nothing, and yet possessing all things. For the word of the Lord is a double-edged sword, turning this way and that. Both edges are necessary, both sides of the truth must be blended in experience and character, before we can stand perfect and complete in all the will of God.

There are certain illustrations of the Christian life which please many of us because they chime in with the modern temper and habit of mind. When God's grace is compared to leaven in the meal or to a seed growing in secret, we easily accept and understand the analogy. The ferment which spreads silently through the mass, the germ which is buried underground in the dark and springs up secretly while men sleep—these figures correspond with our present ways of thought, which are all dominated by the notion of development. Nevertheless such figures and parables do not exhaust the New Testament, not do they express the complete ideal of Christian character. Christ spoke indeed of the seed and the leaven and the mysterious new birth ; but He spoke also and not less often in a far different key. He compared Christians to the pungent salt of the earth, and to the gleaming light of the world. In His words we hear of lamps that flash, and trumpets that peal, and weapons that pierce, and a great cry that breaks upon the midnight, and fire from heaven that baptizes and burns. The very fact that we feel less at home among such metaphors warns us that we ought the more heedfully to lay their lesson to heart. Michaelmas, with its awful paradox of war in heaven, declares that the Christian life is not merely a growth, but a battle. *Michael and his angels fought against the dragon*—tells us in the sharpest and most vivid way that those who are the friends of God must be the sworn enemies of Satan. As we love the Lord, we must hate that which is evil. We must not only renounce iniquity, but resist it, and fight against it, and trample it under our feet. To-day, tolerance is one of the most popular virtues ; yet we must search our own hearts to see whether our tolerance be indeed rooted in the Divine Charity, or whether it be a mere confusion between the eternal opposites of right and wrong. Much that people call tolerance is simply easy-going flabbiness ; it proceeds from cowardice and sloth, from our dislike of clear thinking and strong feeling, from our doubt whether most things are worth being angry over, from a lurking suspicion whether anything seriously matters after all. But apart from the hate of hate and the scorn of scorn, no man can fulfil the love of love. How many Christians are holy enough to be as intolerant of evil as Christ was Himself ?

Yet the Christian Church exists as one perpetual protest against the powers of darkness ; it is bound to be a constant offence and alarm to all tyranny and oppression and corruption, whether in high places or in low. So Michaelmas reminds us that we belong to the Church militant—the Church whose normal attitude towards this world's evil is neither compromise nor neutrality, but war.

The Bible proclaims the eternal doom of all things evil, and promises the eternal triumph of all things good. We are apt to think of that triumph rather as a process than as a climax ;

yet it shall come in a moment, in the twinkling of an eye, at the last trump. For *the trumpet shall sound* : and the ancient Church believed that it shall sound from the lips of St. Michael —the great archangel himself being set to herald the supreme victory which he and his host have been used to win. In past ages Christians pictured St. Michael not simply as the militant champion of righteousness, but as having already vanquished all the legions of sin. He is not merely a warrior, but a conqueror. We may imagine him not

"With hostile brow and visage all inflamed,"

but rather, as Perugino pictured him, fair in resistless radiance and calm with the repose of eternal conquest. He stands all-peaceful in the might of God. He is the " vessel and instrument of omnipotence, filled like a cloud with the victor light, the dust of principalities and powers beneath his feet, the murmurs of hell against him heard by his spiritual ear like the winding of a shell on the far-off sea-shore."

Here is the spirit of the Christian soldier, who fights for God on earth even as the angels fight in heaven. His heart is garrisoned by the Almighty Love which casts out fear. He is kept peaceful in the midst of strife. He can be calm with the assurance of final victory. The warrior-saint, who does battle for Christ always, can possess Christ always even in the midst of battle. For this profound paradox is itself double : war—even in heaven ; but, not less surely, heaven—even in war.

THE REAL PRESENCE

THE last recorded words from the lips of Christ on earth are a promise : " Lo, I am with you alway, even unto the end." Before He leaves them, our Lord gives His friends this parting pledge that His absence shall be only apparent. Though the cloud receives Him out of their sight, yet He will be really and truly present with them still, and not with them only but with all generations of the faithful so long as the world shall last. Christ has just uttered His great commission. He has charged His apostles to carry His Gospel to all men's ears. He commands them, in His Name, to undertake the spiritual conquest of mankind. Who else could have conceived such a commission ? Who else could have ratified it with such a promise ? But the two are proportionate and correspondent. The second justifies the first. If Jesus Christ be indeed what Christians have always believed Him to be, then this promise is no poetic figure of speech. The Eternal Son of God can be literally present with the humblest disciple who calls Him Master. He can be actually guiding the fortunes of His Church through the generations of time, moving and working among us to-day though our eyes are holden to His unseen reality.

The doctrine of the Real Presence lies embedded in the core of Christian faith. Here is the central truth of the Gospel—the unbroken personal relation between the Redeemer and His redeemed. Now a physician may invent some remedy which he sends out into the world, and never touches again. A thinker may originate some philosophy which spreads by its inherent truth, without reference to its propounder. A legislator may enact some code which he bequeaths to his people when he has departed. But Christianity exists otherwise ; when once it is detached from the Presence of Christ Himself, it dissolves and waxes old and is ready to vanish away. The Gospel has for its very essence that each believer shall live day by day in conscious fellowship with the One Author and Finisher of faith. Christian theology centres round our Lord's Person, and Christian history is the track of His footsteps on the sands of time.

Read the chequered story of the Church, and judge whether this overwhelming promise has been a dead letter. Weigh the failures of Christianity against its triumphs, and see whether the Church be not only a great thought which every man ought to study, but also a mighty fact which every man is bound to measure. In spite of all errors and corruptions, it is alive to-day, and it keeps the ardour of youth. It has never abandoned its immense task ; it is moving onwards still. A French sceptic once confessed : " Christianity is doubt-less divine, because so many centuries of frauds and follies have not been able to destroy it." But this inexhaustible vitality and energy draw from a hidden Fountain. The Church survives by virtue of Him Whom Bunyan saw in his dream, pouring oil in secret upon the smoulder-ing fire which the world vainly seeks to quench.

Moreover the Real Presence is not only embedded in Christian doctrine and evidenced in Christian history, but affirmed by Christian experience. Study the words and works of the truest Christians—the men so characteristic of their Master that they may be taken as types and examples of faith. Question the great confessors and doctors and missionaries of the Gospel, and they all tell the same tale. In modern days there are many who stumble at the lives of the saints. Let us admit that not a few saints were ignorant and credulous. They indulged in ascetic practices with which we have little sympathy, they lived in a civiliza-tion and mental climate remote from ours, their ways of thinking are out of date. But let us pierce through the husk of their religion to its kernel. When we catch the words they drop unawares, which betray the inwrought habit of the heart, we discover that the secret of their holiness, the power which made them good and kept them good in a wicked world, was nothing else but the supernatural Presence of Jesus Christ Himself as the very bread and light and strength of their souls. Each of them had a passionate devotion to the Person of the Redeemer, a vivid sense of His present reality. It has been finely said that " the Gospels are not four, but ten thousand times ten thousand and thousands of thousands, and the last word of every one of them is *Lo, I am with you alway, even unto the end of the world*."

Listen to the death-cries of the martyrs. In that last extremity a man speaks out of the depths of his nature. And the martyrs spend their parting breath in converse with One Whom they know to be actually present amid their pain. In the awful valley of the shadow they cry out to the Crucified, " Thou art with me." As they pass through the fiery furnace of persecution they recognize their Companion, whose form is like unto the Son of God.

Listen to the psalms of the faithful. The aroma and fragrance of Christian devotion are concentrated in Christian song. What are the greatest hymns of the Church, which echo down through the centuries, those we love best, of which we never grow tired ? They are hymns which affirm or invoke the Real Presence. For as a devout woman wrote : " This is what we want to see—Christ, as it were face to face—to know Him heart with heart."

The Christian life would be hopeless, except for the one thing which makes it attainable. To be a Christian means to do what of ourselves we cannot do, and to choose what naturally we neither desire nor enjoy. But Christ never tells us that we can be His disciples detached from Himself. Our life is created and sustained by His Real Presence dwelling in the members of His Body. He Himself is involved and infused in every movement of a Christian's deepest experience. That experience of faith cannot always be expressed, or even understood ; but it proceeds from nothing less than Christ's own very Person at the springs of our heart and will. It is bound up with the Presence, more real than home and friends, than earth and sun and stars, Who is with us always, Who will be with us while days and years are counted, even unto the end.

WHEN I AM WEAK, THEN AM I STRONG

ST. PAUL sums up in his own person the paradox of Christian experience. We need not speculate about the precise nature of that thorn or stake in the flesh which he endured. His self-disclosure points to something acutely painful, something purely physical, something terribly humiliating, something which he knew he would never be rid of. Moreover the apostle recognized that it was sent to him as an antidote against spiritual pride. It came " by reason of the exceeding greatness of the revelation," as a counterpoise to that dazzling weight of glory. In Raphael's picture of the Transfiguration one frame and one canvas include the vision on the holy mount above and the convulsed demoniac struggling on the plain below. In St. Paul's experience the unspeakable rapture and the humbling anguish are compressed into the same person. Like Alfred the Great with his cancer, like William of Orange with his fragile health, the apostle fulfilled his mission, wrestling against feebleness of flesh and blood day by day. Pain can be faced and conquered when it only comes occasionally. But to find yourself disfigured, or injured, or crippled for life ; to discover that the mischief is cureless, and that you must go on suffering without any real respite ; to know that you will have to creep on broken wing for all the rest of the way, until the end— this is what human nature revolts and rebels against. The terrible cross to carry is the cross which you must carry permanently without any hope of relief, the cross which in this world God refuses to let you lay down.

Yet the holiest and most apostolic men, with richest gifts and rarest insight, are perhaps most in danger of spiritual pride. And against this deadliest and subtlest of temptations God's chosen safeguard is ofttimes the steady, ceaseless pressure of some humbling, distressing pain. Not seldom He maims and cripples what we call a career of Christian usefulness, in order that He may perfect a saint in secret submission and child-like dependence of soul. The outward hindrance is sent as an inward help. The physical stumbling-block becomes a spiritual stepping-stone. The weary load is transformed into " such a burden as wings are to a bird or sails to a ship." What we count as messengers of Satan prove angels of God in disguise. And when He gives His angels charge concerning us to keep us back from the gateway of social or ecclesiastical success, it is a charge that in their hands they shall bear us up to that paradise which He hath prepared for them that love Him.

St. Paul tells us how he besought the Lord thrice that his cross might depart from him. Yet the fervent prayer of this righteous man did not avail for the end he desired. But in a far deeper sense it was answered and fulfilled by the presence, the voice, the all-sufficient grace of Christ Himself. Grace in the New Testament implies spiritual energy, infused into the soul. Grace carries with it Christ's own courage and fortitude, and the patience that endures to the end, and the victory that overcomes the world. And in the paradox of Christian experience we can receive this grace most effectually only when we need it most utterly, when we are broken down into sheer poverty of spirit. Those who are shipwrecked helplessly on God obtain such Divine succours as no one else can ever understand. *When I am weak, then am I strong*, is the confession of the children of grace in all generations. Man's extremity becomes God's precise opportunity. Our bitterest pain proves to be a sacrament of heavenly com-

fort.   The body of our humiliation is made into
an avenue for the manifestation of Divine love.

Who can understand or describe the unspeakable compensations which Christ grants to
those disciples from whom He seems to take
away so much which we count worth having ?
In the economy of grace it is the bruised lives
and the shattered plans and the broken health
and the spilled spikenard which are peculiar
objects of the Lord's blessing.   His angels
excel in strength ; but His saints excel in
weakness.   His apostles conquer through
infirmities and necessities and distresses.   His
little flock, when it is most minished and
brought low, receives the kingdom unawares.
When the Church is weak, then it is strong.
What we call its hindrances are appointed as
its helps.   Suffering and impoverished and
buffeted, it becomes once more the vessel and
instrument of Omnipotence.   When other
helpers fail and comforts flee, Christians know,
as they never knew before, that underneath are
the Everlasting Arms.

LOVEST THOU ME ?

THE restoration of Simon Peter after he had
thrice denied his Master could not be completed
until one question had pierced his heart like a
sword.   That same question, *Lovest thou Me ?*
still probes and searches and judges every man
who names the Name of Christ.   Here is His

supreme requirement, His final test. In the eyes of Jesus the one thing needful is that we should be bound by passionate personal attachment to Himself. Measured against this, any other standard appears of small account. It is amazing to realize how our Lord has reduced religion and morality to their simplest elements. *Lovest thou Me ?* is His sole test for discipleship. He deliberately stakes everything on this single qualification. It seems that in His judgment nothing else seriously matters compared with one master-passion of the soul. *Lovest thou Me ?*—will there be any other question for a man to answer at the last assize ?

Half the mistakes which we make in theology are due to our habit of thinking and arguing about spiritual facts as if they were no more than abstract terms. But in God's revelation of Himself, He is continually translating the abstract into the concrete. Indeed, we can receive His revelation in no other way. " Ideas are often poor ghosts ; they pass athwart us in thin vapour. But sometimes they are made flesh ; they breathe upon us with warm breath, they touch us with soft responsive hands, they look at us with sad sincere eyes, and speak to us in appealing tones ; they are clothed in a living human soul, with all its conflicts, its faith, and its love. Then their presence is a power, then they shake us like a passion, and we are drawn after them with gentle compulsion, as flame is drawn to flame." It is not too much

to say that sacred words like duty and holiness,
repentance and forgiveness, convey no proper
meaning, they are without form and void, so
long as they remain abstractions.   They become
alive and real only in relation to living persons.
Because, as Bishop Creighton used to say, life
itself is the development of personality.   What
makes you in this world ?   Your relations to
other persons.   Relationships founded on a
sense of lasting affection are the sole realities
of life.   Faith means nothing else than personal
trust in another person.   Love itself is a mere
label, until you kindle with the glow of affection
for some other person.   So even Almighty God
can come near to us and make Himself known
to us, when He is found in fashion as a Man.
And the appeal of Jesus Christ to each man
carries this intimate personal challenge :   *Lovest
thou Me ?*

When we consider the witness of Christian
experience, we begin to understand how our
Lord's question penetrates to its characteristic
quality and essence.   A Christian is a person
who is in love with Christ.   Behind and beneath
questions about orthodoxy or institutions, here
lies the root of the matter.   No heresy can be so
deadly, no sin can be so black, as a hard,
loveless, cynical heart.   On the other hand, as
an ancient Father was bold to say, the touch of
love can supersede all sacraments.   Yet how
rarely we reckon those Christians to be in the
front rank of the Church who are distinguished

by nothing else except their immense power of affection. We still reserve the chief seats in our synagogues for the eloquent speakers, the munificent givers, the superior people who certainly are not pre-eminent for simple, un-wearying, self-forgetful tenderness. But, after all, the best Christian is he who has the deepest personal love for Christ.

There is no other secret of effectual Christian service. It was the reality of Simon Peter's affection which furnished the only valid proof of his fitness for his apostolic work. We can never feed Christ's lambs or shepherd His sheep or preach His Gospel to any real purpose, unless our effort be inspired by a profound, ardent passion of love for Christ Himself. He demands of us first and foremost, not that we be cumbered with much serving, but that we set Him on the pedestal of our hearts, giving a lower place to all other objects of devotion and desire. The very form of the charge to Simon Peter, " Feed My sheep," warned him not to think of the flock except as being Christ's own possession. We cannot even teach a Sunday-school class properly so long as we do it from a sense of public duty, or from an interest in the charm of childhood, or for any other motive except love for the Eternal Shepherd Who stands in the midst of the little ones and says, " My lambs."

For lack of this one thing needful how much of our religious effort degenerates, until it becomes at last a barrenness or a bondage. But those disciples whose hearts are aflame with love for Christ discover that their reward is with them every day they live. Take one example only. Listen to David Livingstone making his way alone across the deserts of unexplored Africa. In a letter dated September, 1843, he wrote : " That hymn of St. Bernard, on the name of Christ, rings in my ears as I wander across the wide, wide wilderness : *Jesu dulcis memoria*—' Jesus, the very thought of Thee with sweetness fills my breast.' " The truest Christians—perhaps we ought to say, the only true Christians—are those who have found it possible to conceive for Jesus Christ an attachment the closeness of which no words can describe, a veneration so possessing and so absorbing the man within them that they have said, " I live no more, but Christ lives in me." Day by day they look up wistfully for His smile, they shrink like children from His tenderest reproach. For their greatest grief would be to grieve Him ; and their chief desire is that, whether by their living or their dying, Christ shall be well pleased.

LISTENING FOR THE LORD

THE Bible is the record of how God has continually been trying to make Himself understood, to explain what His nature really is and

what He cares about and what He demands.
Yet to creatures such as we are, amid these
earthly shadows and confusions, God could
only reveal Himself gradually. Of old He spake
by the prophets at sundry times and in divers
manners, as men were able to bear it ; and
even then Israel often missed His meaning, they
failed to comprehend the syllables of the Divine
speech. Finally God manifested Himself once
for all in the Person of His Son. The Eternal
Word was made flesh and dwelt among us, and
entered into our human lot, and shared all our
struggles and sorrows, and drank our bitterest
cup, and bore away the sin of the world.

Yet the people who lived with Jesus Christ
and walked by His side and listened to Him
day by day never properly understood Him. It
was not possible for Him to make Himself fully
known. They were not able to bear it. Those
faithful men and women who companied with
our Lord across the hills of Galilee, and hung
on His lips in the market-place and synagogue—
how could they take in all the meaning of His
mighty words ? How could they measure the
Master Whom half-blindly they adored ? Much
therefore He spoke to them in mystic figures
and parables, and many things He left unsaid.
He was content to be Himself—to live His life
and utter His message and endure His Passion
and offer His sacrifice and win His victory—
and then, from the right hand of God, to move
by His Spirit in the hearts and memories of

those disciples who first began to know Him after He had passed out of their sight.

The New Testament forms a commentary on Christ's warning to His disciples : " I have many things to say unto you, but ye cannot bear them now." It shows us, for example, how He, Who is Himself the Truth, was yet constrained to teach with a certain economy and reserve. This, indeed, belonged to the Lord's humiliation, whereby for our sakes He became poor. The Light of the world must needs suffer eclipse and obscurity, because men's dim eyes could not bear its unshaded splendour. And even out of our own experience we can partly understand this necessity. For are we not driven to practise the same kind of reserve with our own children ? We have many things to say unto them, but they cannot bear them now. So we use fairy tales and fables and parables, and we keep much unspoken. Because it would be foolish and hurtful to speak to a child about matters which only concern mature men and women. In teaching the Gospel to simple souls there is a corresponding restraint to be observed. Experienced missionaries deal in this way with their young converts at the outset. So St. Paul felt compelled to temper his message for those whom he called " babes " in spiritual truth. But the same great apostle exhorts us to grow in the knowledge of our Lord and Saviour. For all true knowledge must needs be a growth. Every wise teacher

discovers that merely " saying things " is idle
work ; his pupils listen, and then whisper to
each other, " What is this ? We cannot tell
what he saith." Similarly as we grow older, we
come to understand love and friendship only
by slow degrees. Few of us appreciate our
fathers and mothers while we live with them at
home. Their wonderful affection is half hidden
from us, until we begin to realize it when we
have children of our own. All life's deep
realities must be learned in the same fashion.
With endless, tireless patience God goes on
trying to make us understand His unutterable
Secret, trying to reveal Himself to our spirits
day by day.

Some of us suppose that we comprehend
Jesus Christ. We adopt the orthodox theory as
to His Person. We believe the apostolic doctrine of His place in the spiritual order of
things. We accept broadly the teaching of the
Reformers about the redemption He wrought.
We share the modern sympathy with His
compassion for the heavy-laden and the poor.
But assuredly our Lord has still many things to
say unto us which we have never understood
as yet. Not a few of His simplest commands we
read, and ignore. Points in His plainest teaching we hear, and pass over absently or muse
on in a kind of bewilderment. Some of His
greatest precepts and promises have never
controlled our consciences or possessed our
hearts. We " cannot bear them " ; we admit

that Christ spoke those strange words, but " we cannot tell what He saith."

Listen to our Lord's astonishing sayings about the duty of forgiveness—how He absolutely forbids us to avenge our personal wrongs. Has the Church as a whole ever faced those sayings or put them into practice ? Yet they imply a hidden Divine power in gentleness and meekness and pity which can quell and conquer the wrath and violence of men. Consider, again, Christ's teaching about purity and the redemption of the impure. He declared that love can reclaim the fallen, however darkly their souls and bodies are defiled. Magdalene herself may be restored to whiteness, and her vile past made as though it had never been. Can we yet bear that hard saying ? Do we believe in such a miracle of the grace of God ? Consider, again, Christ's words of warning against wealth and in praise of poverty. Do we exhaust them when we limit their meaning to poverty of spirit ? Is there not something beyond—a beatitude which belongs to literal renunciation and detachment and denial— which the saints of God have recognized but from which we habitually turn away our eyes ? And sayings such as these are no stray sentences of doubtful authority, no new *logia* unearthed from some Egyptian tomb. They belong to the core of our Lord's message. Do they not make us feel how many things He has to say to *us*, which we never yet have been able to receive ?

The one thing final about the Gospel is Jesus Christ Himself—the same yesterday and to-day and for ever. But that very verse translates Him out of the past into the present. It means that He goes on teaching His disciples now, as certainly as He taught them of old in the days of His flesh. " All the words He ever spake, still to us He speaketh." By His Spirit within us He is still guiding and enlightening and inspiring each willing and obedient heart. There was a little child who used to come eagerly to her father morning by morning with the same request, " Please tell me something " ; and when he asked, " Something about what ? " the child always answered, " Something you have not told me before." If we lived in that happy wistful expectancy, we should not miss the fresh messages and new meanings that are in store for a child-like heart—a heart which listens for the Divine Voice and makes answer, " Speak, Lord, for Thy servant heareth."

FOR THIS CAUSE WE FAINT NOT

ENDURANCE is one of the chief watchwords of the New Testament—endurance, which is the final loyalty of faith. " For this cause we faint not " seemed to St. Paul almost the loftiest confession he could utter ; and the apostle set before his converts as their supreme ideal, " having done all, to stand." The Epistle to the Hebrews enforces this high and precious

19

virtue of spiritual constancy. And the Epistle
of James is full of warnings to the impatient
and the unstable ; while again and again it
counts them happy that endure. In the
Apocalypse our Lord Himself takes the same
tone and accent when He speaks to His Church
at Ephesus : " Thou hast borne, and hast
patience, and for My Name's sake hast laboured,
and hast not fainted." In each of the seven
Churches Christ's blessing is reserved for him
that overcometh, and " keepeth My words
unto the end."

Our homely English proverbs admonish us
that to begin is not the same as to finish. And
assuredly this principle applies to the Christian
life. It is not enough that in the morning we
have faith to choose the good part, that we
dedicate ourselves at daybreak to seek the
enduring treasure and the immortal prize.
Young disciples, from the nature of the case,
cannot possibly realize all that such a choice
involves. They have no calculus to measure
how much it costs to be a Christian.

> " Let no man think that sudden, in a minute,
>   All is accomplished, and the work is done ;
>   Though with thine earliest dawn thou should'st begin it,
>   Scarce were it ended with thy setting sun."

Therefore, besides the courage of decision, we
need the far harder courage of continuance as
well. Professor A. B. Davidson used to say
that to his mind the saddest sentence in the
whole Bible was this : " Even the youths shall

faint and be weary, and the young men shall utterly fall." Every teacher has seen the words come true of some brilliant student. Every minister has had to mourn over splendid spiritual promise which endured for a season and then, because it had no root, withered away. We need not appeal to the theologians on this question. Ask the poets whether inconstancy be not a deadly defect in character. The man who is fickle in temper, capricious in taste, infirm of purpose, vacillating in resolve, is the typical example of weakness portrayed in half the dramas and the novels ; while inconstancy of a deeper kind leads straight on to misery and moral ruin. We recognize that a true hero must at any rate possess tenacity and persistence ; he must be staunch to his friends at all hazards, he must follow his star faithfully at all costs, he must play the game out to the very finish. While on the other hand we recognize the fatal streak in the nature of the man who does not endure to the end. We call him deserter, or backslider, or apostate, or renegade. He belongs to the lost legion of those who were once enlightened but made the great refusal.

What is the secret of spiritual endurance ? When Adam Bede was describing the career of Moses he summed up the history of the Hebrew captain in a quaintly simple sentence : " Moses carried a hard business well through." And the Bible tells us the secret : " he endured, as

seeing Him Who is invisible." Nothing else
but the continual vision of Him Who is invisible
can keep us all our lives through steadfastly
loyal to the good part, undaunted by the
tyranny of things temporal, unbeguiled by the
delusions of things seen. The discerning of
Almighty God, and His will, and His judgments,
day by day—this alone can secure us against
the snares of the world and sustain us under
its burdens. Only the great White Throne
glimmering through these mortal shadows can
fix our eyes on the moral value of things and
the final recompense of reward. But we can
endure, as seeing Him Who is invisible—Him
Whom having not seen we love, in Whom,
though now we see Him not, yet believing, we
rejoice even now with joy unspeakable and full
of glory.

This truth applies to constancy in our
Christian service. Some of us have proved
how manifold are the discouragements and disappointments which such service involves. To
be deceived by those you trust and betrayed by
those you care for, to be hindered and thwarted
and misunderstood by the very people you are
most anxious to befriend—these are experiences
which no loyal Christian can escape. Our
secret of endurance lies in considering Him Who
endured such contradiction of sinners against
Himself, lest we grow weary and faint in our
minds. Nay, the contradiction of sinners is
sometimes less heart-breaking than the con-

tradition of saints—the criticism and hostility and contempt which you suffer at the hands of religious persons because you cannot pay them and their methods the flattery of imitation. Consider Him Who endured it all. Our Lord's divine patience shone out most wonderfully, not in His dealings with publicans and sinners, but in His encounters with righteous men who needed no repentance.

Moreover we must have grace to endure, if we are to profit by our portion in God's fatherly chastisement. Is there any sterner verse in Scripture than this : " He scourgeth *every* son whom He receiveth " ? Is there any sharper trial of faith than to bow your head and confess humbly, " It pleased the Lord to bruise me " ? Great troubles sometimes embitter the soul that rebels against them and refuses to be exercised thereby. Only to those who patiently endure God's chastening does it yield the peaceable fruit of righteousness. Often we can discover no explanation of a calamity or a bereavement. Again and again in these tragic years we have had simply to say, " It has pleased the Lord. . . . It is His doing, though it is terrible in our eyes." But God's elect sufferers learn the last secret of endurance when they commit the keeping of their souls to Him, as to a faithful Creator. Even though we are faithless, He abideth faithful. The final perseverance of His children is rooted in the perseverance of God. The Old Testament shows us how Israel exulted

in this glorious certainty. " The goodness of
God endureth for ever," they sang ; " His truth
endureth unto all generations." And the New
Testament is the revelation of One Who lets
men suffer, and yet comes to suffer with them ;
One Who lets men die, and yet comes to die
for them ; One Who does not overwhelm injustice but Himself undergoes it all. Because He
is Himself the changeless, tireless Love that
beareth all things, and endureth all things, and
never faileth.

Endurance is the final loyalty of faith. We
can endure to the end, as seeing Him Who is
Himself our Beginning and our End, our First
and our Last.

THE GIFT OF THE MORNING STAR

FEW promises, even in the Apocalypse, are so
difficult to translate into experience as the
mystic words : *I will give him the morning star.*
For this saying comes to us clothed in a metaphor
for which we can find no precise definition, no
complete interpretation. Holy Scripture was
written in lands where the heaven above is far
more lucid and radiant than in our misty English
latitude ; where the planets shine clearer and
men look up at larger constellations burning in
the midnight sky. This fact, borne in mind
when we read the Bible, illuminates its references to the lights which God has kindled in

the firmament for signs and seasons. To Syrian shepherds, keeping watch over their flocks through the darkness, the morning star does not merely glimmer, it glows and blazes above the horizon to prophesy the dawn. In all ages this star has shone as a harbinger which bears witness that the night is far spent and the day is at hand. It is the day-star of hope.

At a time like the present, which is so clouded and thick with discouragements, we need above all else to confirm our confidence in Christ Who is our hope. For in truth we have lived through a long midnight. We have kept vigil through black and bitter hours which were haunted with unseen terrors. Year after year we endured the strain of war, and its havoc and its grief. And since war ended in victory we have had to pass through all the disillusions and disappointments which followed in the train of peace. Even now men's hearts fail them for fear, and for looking after those things which are coming on the earth. It seems sometimes as though a torrent of change were sweeping over our sacred landmarks. What Mr. John Galsworthy calls " the Victorian dykes " have broken down, and the waters are rolling in like a flood upon property and morals and manners and the old forms of art. Even within the citadel of faith itself we encounter confusion and dismay invading the Church of God. On the threshold of the new era nothing is more needed by Christ's dejected people than that He should fulfil His promise of this gift of the morning star.

It is natural enough for young men and maidens to be light-hearted. With their buoyant vitality they can be hopeful by happy instinct. Such eager expectancy is the prerogative of youth ; very few remain sanguine after their hair turns grey. But the Christian hope which maketh not ashamed means far more than natural high spirits or sunny temperament. Indeed, some of the truest saints have had to fight against constitutional depression. In the *Pilgrim's Progress* Bunyan deals tenderly with Despondency and his daughter Much-afraid, who were rescued from the dungeons of Giant Despair's castle. But his favourite character of all seems to have been Mr. Fearing. When we read that wonderful autobiography, *Grace abounding to the Chief of Sinners*, we understand how many touches in the portrait of Mr. Fearing were taken from Bunyan's own experience. Concerning this pilgrim we are told that he lay at the Slough of Despond for above a month, till one sunshiny morning he ventured and got over ; and when he was over, he would scarce believe it. He stood shaking and shrinking at the wicket-gate, but would not go back again. " It would have pitied one's heart to have seen him." In the Interpreter's House he had more comfort ; for the Interpreter, being very tender to them that are afraid, carried it wonderful lovingly to him. He was glad and cheery at the sight of the Cross and Sepulchre, and made no stick at the Hill Difficulty. He was never better than in the Valley of Humiliation, and would lie down, embrace the ground, and kiss the flowers that grew there. In the Valley of the Shadow he was ready to die with fear : but Greatheart " took very great notice that this Valley was as quiet while he went through it as ever I knew it before or since." At Vanity Fair he would have fought with all the men in the Fair, so hot was he against their fooleries ; and upon the Enchanted Ground he was very wakeful. But at the River he was in a heavy case, for now, now he would be drowned for ever, and so never see that Face with comfort that he had come so many miles to behold. Yet it was very remarkable that the River was lower at this time than it had ever been in the memory of man, and so he went over at last not much above wet-shod.

Mr. Fearing must have lived in Bedford. Indeed, these timid and troublesome pilgrims can be found in every congregation. Through God's tireless patience they persevere to the end ; but they are very far indeed from becoming leaders. On the other hand, we do meet certain rare spirits who are endowed with the grace of unconquerable optimism. These are the dauntless captains and pioneers of God's cause, and their lamps shine brightest in gloom. When others quail, such a one will cry : " Be of good cheer." He strengthens the weak hands, and confirms the feeble knees. Within his breast he carries the gift of the morning star, and darkness flees before him.

Very few of us are born for leadership. Nevertheless, each believer can claim his portion in this mystic promise. We shall not err if we explain it by those other words of Him Who uttered it, and Who has testified concerning Himself : " I am the bright and morning star." For the supreme gift which Christ bestows is the gift of Himself. Of Him and through Him and to Him are all things. Here is the blessing which embraces and includes every other. To possess His awful and glorious Presence dwelling in the soul—this is the one sure and certain hope which makes despair and defeat impossible : " this is alone love, joy, empire, victory."

OUR LORD'S LEGACY

WHEN the Eternal Son, Who for our sakes became poor, entered on the evening of His earthly day, He was homeless and naked of possessions. Already in spirit He had made the sacrifice of Himself, He had given His Body and His Blood for the life of the world. It seemed that He had nothing to call His own which He might bequeath to His friends before He went away. Yet in His last testament He left them one ineffable legacy : *Peace I leave with you, My peace I give unto you.* Now plainly such words point to something which

lies beyond the initial act of pardon in which
Christian experience begins. When Christ
speaks of " the peace that is Mine," He is not
thinking of any assurance of sins forgiven.
He means that absolute calm which belongs to
His own Being, which He bestows on the men
whom He makes partakers of the Divine
nature. By virtue of this bequest He intends
His disciples to share His life of tranquillity,
through all the tumult and the pain of time.

In old-fashioned evangelical circles there used
to be a familiar test-question : " Have you
found peace ? " Many persons who have called
themselves Christians for half a lifetime are
confronted by another test-question : " Have
you retained peace ? " Sometimes we are
tempted to tell ourselves in despair that it is
not possible for anyone to preserve inner
quietness of spirit amid the trouble and bewilderment of such a restless generation as
ours. Is it a fact that we have lost our inheritance in Christ's great legacy to His redeemed ? Are we, at any rate, missing our
full portion in the perpetual promise, " Ye shall
find rest unto your souls " ?

It is true that there may often be special
circumstances and personal conditions which
combine to break and spoil a Christian's inward
stillness. His temperament, perchance, is eager
and impatient ; or his disposition is peevish
and sullen ; or his health is indifferent and his
nerves are jangled out of tune ; or his daily

work is harassing and disappointing ; or his associates are a constant irritation ; or his future prospects are anxious and overcast. Nevertheless the peace of God which passeth all understanding can so garrison our hearts that none of these things shall disturb the central citadel. Only an hour before He went out to His agony and betrayal, the Lord looked round on His perplexed and foreboding friends and said serenely : *My peace I give unto you.*

Because peace, in the Christian sense of the word, does not mean stoical passivity or sentimental self-absorption :

> " Not peace that grows by Lethe, scentless flower,
> There in white languors to decline and cease ;
> But peace whose names are also rapture, power,
> Clear sight and love ; for these are parts of peace."

The peace which Christ bestows out of His own fullness is the poise and harmony of all ardours and passions, of all our powers with all their might, made one with the will of God. And this beatitude is not brought about as the result of our struggle and endeavour : it descends as a gift from above. Christ's authentic peace comes down to abide in every soul which is surrendered to His love. It follows as a sequel and result of the mystical union which incorporates the redeemed in their Redeemer. The essential life of the Vine flows out into the branches. Our peace belongs to our life, which is hid with Christ in God.

In this generation the distractions and com-

petitions of the world have infected the mission
of the Church. Numbers of Christians, for
example, dissipate and fritter away their souls
among a multitude of religious activities and
interests. They are careful and troubled about
many things. Whereas one supreme secret of
inward repose is to withdraw from the circum-
ference of faith and to dwell steadily at its
Centre—according to the promise, " Thou wilt
keep him in perfect peace whose mind is stayed
on Thee." Moreover, the common snare which
besets believers to-day is to toil and strain in
breathless, feverish fashion at what they call
" Christian work "—as though either they
themselves or the world around them had to
be redeemed by human efforts and sacrifices.
No real success in spiritual service is achieved
except by those workers in whose hearts rests
the covenant of peace. And it is characteristic
of this peace that it is rooted and grounded in
the Divine Work, in an Action and a Passion
outside ourselves and beyond all our moods of
feeling. The only message which can speak to
the heart of Jerusalem is the message which
assures her not only that her iniquity is pardoned, but also that in very truth her warfare
is accomplished by the victory of the Son of
God.

This supernatural peace proves the final
antidote to all our anxiety and despondency
and dismay. In the slow, sad experience of
life a Christian is in no wise exempted from

losses and failures. It may be that he must watch the argosy of his earthly hopes and plans suffer shipwreck : yet the Lord is faithful Who has promised, not " I will give thee success," but " I will give thee rest." Or he may find himself bereft and desolate and haunted with the dread of bleak, solitary old age. Time, the subtle thief of youth, may rob him in the end of most things, except that peace which the world can neither give nor take away. As we gaze down the shadowy avenue of our own future, who would not quail to imagine the dark possibilities which it may conceal, if he did not hear the Voice which still whispers : " My peace I give unto you : let not your heart be troubled, neither let it be afraid."

> " Hereat, my soul, go softly ; not for long
> Runs thy still hour from prime till evensong ;
> Come shine or storm, rejoice thee or endure,
> Set is thy course and all thy haven is sure ;
> Nor guide be thine thro' halcyon seas or wild
> Save the child's heart and trust as of the child."

A GRAIN OF WHEAT

FEW sights are lovelier or more suggestive than a field of ripe wheat, dyed with the colour of sunshine and rippling into a thousand touches of tawny gold. This year we have stood among the corn with strange, new thoughts. For we have come to realize how quickly mankind would starve, were it not for God's recurring bounty in harvest. Now, as never before, we give thanks for the blessing of our daily bread. "A wheat-sack stands open in the market— you can thrust your hand in it a foot deep, or take up a handful and let it run back like a liquid stream, or hold it in your palm and balance it, feeling the weight." They are not very heavy, these little grains ; and yet, as Richard Jefferies perceived with the insight of genius, "wherever they are, there is empire. Could imperial Rome have only grown sufficient wheat in Italy to feed her legions, Cæsar might still be master of civilization." Rome, with her power and glory, is a legend now ; but still the lords of the earth are they who, like Joseph in Egypt, hold the keys of its granaries. To-day, as in ancient times, the struggle between nations is still for the ownership or for the control of corn. The harvest-fields remain the real battle-fields of the world.

Scripture is full of the mingled poetry and mystery which are wrapped up in the miracles of seed-time and harvest. Again and again it brings out the analogies between the visible world and the invisible—analogies which are not merely illustrations, but actual arguments and witnesses for the unseen ; because they depend on that deep vital harmony which subsists between the natural and the spiritual orders, and which reveals them both as different aspects of the same Life. Christ Himself was equally at home in the Bible and in the book of nature. He handled both volumes as though

He were One with their Author; and He points us repeatedly to the spiritual lessons of sowing and reaping. Consider those wonderful words, spoken at Jerusalem in Passion week, with which He welcomed certain Greek pilgrims who sought to see Him at the feast. Our Lord was deeply moved by these men from heathen lands outside Jewry, who came pressing into the presence of their Redeemer. He hailed them with solemn joy as a warning that the hour was come when the Son of Man should be glorified. Yet glorified, not after the fashion of the rulers of this world, but according to the secrets of the Divine counsel. For the glory of the Son of Man consisted in drawing all men unto Himself by His Cross, and in rising through death to the life which is life indeed. *Verily I say unto you, except a grain of wheat fall into the ground and die, it abideth alone : but if it die, it bringeth forth much fruit.*

Surely it is remarkable to find our Lord comparing Himself to one poor solitary grain of wheat. Christ's humbleness is in nothing more conspicuous than in the manner in which He Himself refers to His humiliation. We have many old tales and legends in which the central figure is some prince in disguise. But in such stories the prince never fails to betray that he feels his position to be incongruous, he chafes at his mean garments, he shows that he is not at home in his low estate. When Jesus Christ entered this world of ours He moved along its lowest paths with perfect naturalness. It never seemed to strike Him as a strange thing that He should be poor and despised and rejected. Never was there one trace of condescension in the human accents of the Son of God. To-day, the war has been teaching us many lessons. Yet when we fret against some menial service, when we stoop not without self-conscious embarrassment to render help to the needy, when we mix constrainedly with other helpers whom we think of as our inferiors, then is the time to consider Him Who though He was rich for our sakes became poor, and carried His poverty like a crown : then is the time to pray for true humbleness of heart—the highest virtue, mother of them all. As we look at the ear of wheat which Christ holds in His hand and listen to the words in which He compares Himself to one single grain, we begin to feel how much grace we need before we can follow the example of His great humility.

Further, our Lord takes this grain of wheat— dead and buried out of sight, and thereby springing up into fruitfulness—to be a parable of His own dying, and rising again in the power of an endless life. St. Paul applies the same image to illustrate the mystery of the resurrection of the body. Christ uses it rather as an example of the incalculable fruitfulness of sacrifice. For what is it that happens when a grain of wheat falls into the ground ? " The buried seed," says a wise teacher, " gives itself

20

up, it surrenders itself, it yields before the
forces of nature. They enter into it and take
possession of it, and seem to put it aside and to
blot it out altogether. But that seed comes
again in glory in the harvest. It comes again,
because it has been made one with nature
herself, penetrated and embraced by her energies,
and filled with her fullness, and multiplied by
her life." Now these things are an allegory of
the spiritual order. They show us—to quote
Lacordaire's favourite words—that there is
nothing fruitful except sacrifice. And the self-
same law of sacrifice, which reigns on the
throne of heaven, governs the dullest and
darkest soul on earth. To be self-contained
and self-centred means, spiritually, to abide
alone, and therefore to perish. So Christ went
on to warn those Greek pilgrims in words which
He had often used before : " He that loveth
his life shall lose it ; and he that hateth his life
in this world shall keep it unto life eternal."
Amid tears and anguish and shedding of blood,
we are learning to recognize the spiritual law
of sacrifice, which runs like a scarlet thread
through Scripture. We are beginning to believe
that self-devotion is higher than self-indulgence,
and that to die for a just cause is better than to
live for pleasure. The grain of wheat which
gives itself up, so that it may become seed of
living bread for the hungry, warns us all never
to be afraid of self-surrender. Here is the secret
of inward progress. Only as we abandon, can

we ever attain—and attain manifold more than it has entered into our hearts to conceive. When our Lord takes a single grain of wheat, and shows us its destiny through self-surrender and death to eternal fruitfulness, He is proclaiming afresh the miraculous energy of self-sacrificing love,

" That moves the sun in heaven and all the stars."

NOW IS OUR SALVATION NEARER

ONE deep note of the primitive Church was the note of expectancy. The early believers were full of forward-looking thoughts. Almost the only fragment of a liturgy which the New Testament preserves is the watch-word *Maranatha*—" the Lord cometh," and that word echoed in Christian assemblies and found response in the hearts of the faithful. For they believed not only that Christ had come, and had suffered and conquered and ascended into heaven : they believed also that Christ would speedily come again with great power and glory, to make an end of sin and to deliver His people out of the present evil world. The first disciples laboured and endured and triumphed in the patience of this mighty hope. The most wonderful and blessed of events, the crown and consummation of all things, must happen soon ; it might happen at any moment. And so morning by morning they whispered, " He may be here before sunset " ; and evening by evening

they made answer, " He shall surely come, and
not tarry." The New Testament closes with
the promise, " Behold, I come quickly," ratified
by the happy prayer, " Even so, come, Lord
Jesus."

There were Christians indeed who lost their
balance and grew half distraught at the prospect
of this awful joy, hanging so close above them
and ready so soon to fall. To such St. Paul
wrote grave words of warning ; and in his later
epistles he plainly postponed the advent until
after his own exodus. But in every age the
Church has cherished the same quenchless hope.
Faithful souls in each generation watched wistfully for the day of the Lord, and loved His
appearing. They reaffirmed the ancient faith,
" We believe that Thou shalt come " ; and they
died, not having received the promise, but having
been persuaded of it and embraced it from afar.
Indeed the contrast between the Church's
expectation and its perpetual disappointment
has become a stumbling-block to not a few
believers. Does not history in this matter
give the lie to faith ? Christ has never come
again, in the fashion in which His first disciples
expected to behold Him, before they should
taste of death.

The key to the contradiction, as a wise
teacher suggested, may lie in our human
infirmity. We have no skill to harmonize
things that are temporal with things that are
eternal. Because of the illusion of these mortal

years we are forced to think of a past and of a future which have no place in God's everlasting Now.   It may be that each generation wakes up to discern Christ's advent, as each member of it opens his eyes in the article of death and realizes the spiritual judgment being enacted on earth already.   The day of the Lord may be extending down through all centuries, and yet His manifestation may arrive at successive moments to successive souls as they pass— until the evening of human history, in the sunset of the world's last day.   At any rate this much is certain.   When life closes, Christ will appear to each one of us as our Redeemer and our Judge.   He may arrive at any moment, He will surely come soon.   To a Christian the day of the Lord means at least the day when we die ; and the New Testament points forward to it as a day of release and rapture, the gateway of full salvation to a believing soul.

Salvation, indeed, begins as a present reality. It bestows actual forgiveness of sins, and inward peace of conscience, and definite renewal of character.   Here and now it means fellowship with the Father, and the daily imitation of Jesus Christ on earth, and a constant drinking in of love and power from heaven.   Nevertheless this present salvation is not yet made perfect and complete ; its fullness lies waiting in the future.   Just as a tropical plant which seems dwarfed and blighted under our bleak northern skies will blossom into strange luxuriant beauty when you carry it into the glowing sunshine where it is at home ; so human spirits, which have in them the seed of grace, will break out into their blossoming time when they find their true climate in the cloudless presence of God.

Christians have often been reproached for other-worldliness ; but that reproach hardly applies to the modern Church. Do we know anyone who is overmuch preoccupied with dreams of heaven ? Richard Baxter tells us that in winter afternoons, when it began to be too dark to go on with his reading and writing and before the candles were brought in, he used to sit quietly in the twilight meditating on the Saints' Everlasting Rest. Few of us find leisure for such meditations now. We strive for an earthly paradise so eagerly that our prospect is narrowed by its horizon, and we lose sight of the paradise of God. We grow so intent on improving this world that we have little thought to spare for a better country, that is a heavenly. And so we go bankrupt of the powers of the world to come. Our religion lacks one great spring of buoyancy and courage and hope. We do not exult in expectation of that perfect life with God—the life which is life indeed— which is waiting for us, moving to meet us, perchance even now knocking at the door.

To be a Christian is to be drawing nearer daily to the crown of every hope and the fulfilment of every promise. If this immense truth

were as real to us as we know it to be true, if
this glorious and blessed certainty did but
brood over us like the day, it would kindle our
dull souls into a passion of awe and gratitude
and eager joy. Dante understood how many
go astray in the midway of their mortal course,
because it is just then that their cares and
interests become most absorbing and their
energies are engrossed by success, and they lose
the eager, expectant outlook of the faithful
soul. And yet their salvation is nearer now—
ten years, twenty years, thirty years nearer—
than it was once. They have finished so much
of their pilgrimage that comparatively few
miles of the road remain to be trodden. From
the nature of the case they cannot be so very
far from the celestial city. And in that eternal
prospect the things of time show in their true
colours and dwindle into their proper size.
Our rivalries lose their bitterness and our disappointments their sting. Who would grudge
his sacrifice for others, when soon he will no
longer find an altar on which to offer it ? Who
could not endure partings when he knows that
" all our partings are preliminary to the great
Meeting " ?

Sometimes we rebel against the cross which
God Himself has fastened on our shoulders, we
chafe in the narrow chamber where He shuts us
up as His prisoners of hope. But when we cry
" Lord, how long ? " He makes answer to us
that the time is short and is daily shortening.

of this world the heart has to suffer many disillusions and disappointments and betrayals.
Too often our human affection becomes gradually soured and embittered. Our hope grows
weary, our patience is worn out at last. In
the book of memory, one of the most mournful
chapters is the chapter headed " Estrange-
ments." We ourselves change with the chang-
ing years, and our friends find us curiously
altered. We form fresh ties, we barter old
lamps for new, though the new have no magic
charm. And then slowly, in course of time, a
kind of decrepitude may creep over the inward
man. It is as though our very faculty for
affection had somehow shrivelled and contracted. There is some drying up of the springs
of emotion within us. We lose the power to
feel as passionately and intensely and profoundly as we used to feel. But the Divine
Heart is the same yesterday, and to-day, and
for ever, the quenchless, inexhaustible Fountain.
The love of Christ is just as fresh, as eager, as
venturous, as brimming with expectancy, as
when He claimed us at the first. Concerning
Him alone is fulfilled the saying of the Psalmist :
" Thou hast the dew of Thy youth." The
Lover of our souls is now, as He was in the
beginning, and as He ever shall be, world
without end.

Sometimes a man will sit down quietly and
try to cast the horoscope of his own future.
In a dream he gazes wistfully down the slanting

years before him. What can he be quite certain about ? Whom can he entirely count upon ? Dare he in the end absolutely rely upon himself ? Through all the vistas of our veiled and shadowy hereafter there is but one fact utterly certain, only One Love eternally loyal, only One Friend Who was never yet found less than faithful and true. The pledge of our own endurance is bound up with the enduring love of Christ. This is why we can hold fast the beginning of our confidence and rejoice in full assurance of hope, unto the end. The day draws on towards evening, when the lights will burn low for the last act in the drama ; and " the last act," as Pascal said, " is always tragedy : we shall die alone."

> " In that lonely day of death,
> When no man may befriend,
> And the dark angel standeth by,
> And the world is past and gone,
> Let some voice o'er me cry,
> *And having loved His own,*
> *He loved them to the end.*"

Yet again, this word concerning Divine Love testifies to its quality as well as to its duration. In the margin of the English Revised Version we find an alternative rendering given : *Having loved His own, He loved them to the uttermost.* Westcott expounds the translation with singular force. "As Christ loved His disciples, and had proved His love in the past, so now at this extremity, the night before His passion, He forgot Himself and thought only of them. He

carried His affection to the highest pitch. He
loved them to the uttermost, and gave them
His parting pledge and token of everlasting
love." Through our human fellowship one
with another we come to understand by experience how often personal tenderness is checked
and limited, partly in ourselves by a lack of
capacity for loving, and partly in the objects
of our affection by their lack of worthiness and
their imperfect response. In a world like this,
where most people appear shallow-hearted or
narrow-hearted, where we feel ourselves secretly
plagued and crippled by our own self-seeking,
we take refuge in the Divine Love that loves to
the uttermost. By virtue of this prerogative
Christ is able also to save to the uttermost.
This is why He shall receive the uttermost
parts of the earth for His possession. And
does not this also explain why He claims us,
even to the uttermost? For there is nothing
in the universe so exacting as perfect Love,
nothing so inexorable. Just because God has
set His heart upon us with such Divine passion,
He demands that we shall love Him passionately, with all our heart and soul and mind
and strength. He cannot be content with
less than a complete self-surrender, even to the
uttermost farthing.

IN the history of those "killing times" in Scotland under the last two Stuart kings, when multitudes of persecuted Bible-lovers sealed their faith with their blood, we read that two obscure women were hanged at Edinburgh for the crime of attending conventicles. On their way to the scaffold, one of them, a servant girl, twenty years of age, said to her fellow-sufferer : "Come, let us sing the twenty-third Psalm," which they did. The other, Isabel Alison, of Perth, was condemned for having heard a Cameronian preacher and for refusing the test. On the scaffold she said : "Farewell, all created comforts ; farewell, sweet Bible, in which I delighted most, and which has been sweet to me since I came to prison ; farewell, Christian acquaintances. Now into Thy hands I commit my spirit, Father, Son, and Holy Ghost." Whereupon the hangman threw her over.

In the dying words of this dauntless believer we find implied an idea which many Christians apparently take for granted. Those who cherish God's Book as their most precious earthly possession assume that there can be no place for it in heaven. The Bible is their best treasure in this world ; but it must be left behind—it will drop out of sight, and become of no account—in the life of the world to come. Yet, when we consider the matter more deeply, the case appears otherwise. Our Lord Himself has told us little about what lies in store for men after they die. But the solemn parable in which He almost seems to lift the veil contains these penetrating words, spoken to a departed soul : *Son, remember.* Whatever else death takes from us, it will not rob us of our memory. Indeed, personality could hardly survive in any real sense, if it were divorced from recollection. The old Greek legend spoke of Lethe, the river in Hades, one draught of which could wash away all thought of a man's past. But no such water of oblivion is promised in the Christian Gospel. There may await us, rather, the very opposite of Lethe. When the characters in an ancient manuscript have grown dim with age, its lines are sometimes touched with a chemical solution which revives the faded letters into their pristine clearness. So it may be with the defaced manuscripts of the human soul. The river of death will wash out, not our memory, but only our forgetfulness. Now we remember in part : but then shall we know even as we are known.

When we try to bring home to ourselves this tremendous fact of memory in another world, perhaps the first thought which rises up will be this : " How could we endure to be haunted by all the experiences in our own past ? " And there is no answer—no remedy for endless, intolerable remorse—apart from the reversal and retrieval wrought by that Divine Love which casts our sins into the depths of the sea, and swallows up our very guilt in a passion of endless gratitude. Because we believe in the forgiveness of sins, we have faith also that heaven can include memory.

And are there not some things which even in heaven we could not bear to forget? Even in that world we should not be content to lose all tender recollections of this world, with its mingled beauty and sadness, where we learned the way to a better. Among the never-withering flowers of God's paradise we shall sometimes think how the roses used to cluster in an earthly garden. Amid the anthems of the angels above, we shall not forget how on summer mornings the little birds sang here below. Yes, memory will enter into the joy of the perfect life. And surely memory includes recognition : how could you help knowing your mother, if she met you and called you by that name which no one has ever used since you lost her?

It follows that in heaven a Christian will possess and treasure the Bible, as his most sacred recollection. And perhaps it is not irreverent to ask ourselves for a moment in what light the Scriptures will appear to us— then. In his verses to " The Daisy," an English singer anticipates the time

> " When thou art growing over me,
> And I read the Book by the poet's side,
> And look at thee from God's side of thee."

What will it be like, to read the New Testa-

ment by the side of Him Who is the Author and
Finisher of faith ?　What will our human commentaries and expositions amount to, when
death has broken the seals of the Volume
which here they so often obscure ?　How shall
we marvel at our Lord's promises in the presence
of their fulfilment, and understand His Beatitudes
in the glory of the Beatific Vision !　What will
the Psalms sound like, when we sing them no
longer with faltering voices and in a strange
land ?　There are many Psalms indeed, born
in the wilderness, which suit no lips except an
exile's ; but there are others which belong by
proper right to the celestial country.　Mystics
have claimed the hundred and third Psalm, for
example, as the hymn of the saints in paradise ;
and we may confess that this is a psalm for the
spirits of just men made perfect—a song which,
in its fullest meaning, none but the redeemed in
heaven can sing.

Index

A

à Kempis, Thomas, 184
Adam Bede on Moses, 291
Adoration, the issue of worship [*sed qu.*], 138
Alexander, Wm. (Archbishop), 48
Alford, Henry, his epitaph, 52
Alfred the Great, 278
Alison, Isabel, 317
Americans on " God's country," 27
" Amplius," Xavier's watchword, 150 ; the merchant's, 151 ; the saint's, 151
Anonymous writers quoted, 13, 30, 35, 37, 49, 75, 104, 108, 135, 155, 159, 161, 178, 206, 261, 275, 276, 289, 308, 315
Arabian Nights, as illustrative commentary, 81
" Arithmetic, God's," 242–247
" Ark, laid up in the," 237–242
Arnold, Matthew, 47
Ascension Day, its lessons, 97–101, 224–228
Audience, same root as obedience, 35, 138
Augustine, of Hippo, 14, 30, 282

B

" Back to Christ," its full meaning, 227
Barrie, J. M., 233

Baxter, Rd., on high saints and low sinners, 47
his twilight meditations, 310
Beatitudes, the, summarized, 158–159
Bedford, residence of Mr. Fearing, 297
Benhadad, excuses of his staff, 109–110
Bernard, St., Livingstone and his hymn, 284
Bible, the, Heine's opinion of, 13
its influence on style, 13, 14
" at home in," 13–17
grammar and vocabulary of Christians, 14
individual memories of, 15
for commonplace persons, 20
the Book which is alive, 20–24
its converse vital, personal, practical, 22, 23
its profundity, 28–31
unlike every other book, 39
how we may degrade it, 39
its reserve and reticence, 64
full of fighting, patriotism, and atrocities, 71, 216
the text-book of the divine calculus, 242
in heaven, 319
Blake, Wm., 166
Bread, 121–122
Bright, John, 14
Brooks, Phillips, 265

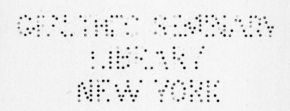
Made and Printed in Great Britain.
Hazell, Watson & Viney, Ld., London and Aylesbury: